Chakra Gardens

Opening the Senses of the Soul

by Carol Cumes

Photography and design by Greg Asbury

additional photographs Keith Levit and Humberto Valdivia

Chakra Gardens: Opening the Senses of the Soul

By Carol Cumes

First Printing © 2008

Mitra Publishing Group
225 North Lima Street
Sierra Madre, California 91024
United States of America

Note to the reader: This book is intended as an informational guide only. The approaches, practices and techniques described herein are not intended to be a substitute for professional medical care or psychiatric treatment. The author makes no representation as to the effectiveness or use of any plant or ritual. Such rituals or practices should only be performed by persons extensively trained in indigenous methods and in the context of that culture.

Various poems throughout the book are from guests of Willka T'ika, all of which are used with permission. All other poetry is of the author.

Text copyright 2008 by Carol Cumes. Chakra Gardens™ mark is the property of the author.

Photography, graphic design and layout copyright 2008 by Greg Asbury, This book was typeset in Helvetica Neue LT Std. with display text Zapfino

additional photos by Keith Levit pp. vi, 2, 30, 104, 106, 135, 206, 229, 240

by Humberto Valdivia pp.6, 31, 36, 59, 115, 120, 146, 157, 182

All photos are reproduced by permission. No other use is permitted

Library of Congress Cataloging-in-Publication Data

Cumes, Carol, 1945-
  Chakra gardens : opening the senses of the soul / Carol Cumes.
    p. cm.
  Includes bibliographical references.
  ISBN 978-0-9654003-9-8 (hardcover)
  1. Gardens--Peru--Religious aspects. 2. Gardening--Religious aspects. 3. Chakras. I. Title.
  BL629.5.G37C86 2008
  299.8'8323--dc22
                            200801558

Printed and bound in China by Palace Press International
10 9 8 7 6 5 4 3 2

ISBN: 978-0-9654003-9-8

additional books may be ordered from www.chakragardens.com

To my children
Lila, Terry, Paul and Romi Cumes,
grandsons Seth and Evan,
and all of Pachamama's Children.

Invitation

In the Andes, Mother Earth is referred to as
Pachamama. Throughout the world, healers,
shamans and sages hear Pachamama's cry to
restore the planet to balance. "First heal the world,
by healing yourself," She whispers, while extending
an invitation to mankind to return to Her gardens. Go
where Nature draws you. Breathe in the energies.
Inhale the fragrant perfumes. Listen deeply, with
your eyes closed, as Pachamama works with you to
provide all you need.

Machu Picchu, the ancient Inkan City of Light, is a short train ride from the Willka T'ika guest house in the Sacred Valley of Peru.

photo courtesy of Keith Levit

Contents

Willka T'ika's Quechua Children's Fund

The spirit of *ayni* is the reciprocal exchange of living energy that occurs through giving offerings and receiving from Mother Earth.

Ayni is an ancient Andean practice that follows the natural principle of balanced giving and receiving. For thousands of years this flow of energy has enabled the Quechua people to endure inhospitable conditions. Practiced in Sacred Valley farming communities surrounding the Chakra Gardens, ayni permeates every aspect of Quechua life. It is one of the richest legacies to have survived in their culture.

With the interest of the Andean Quechua at heart, I developed and offered my support to programs for Quechua children in isolated, mountain schools. To do this, I created the Willka T'ika Children's Fund, a non-profit organization. The Children's Fund has provided school buildings, libraries and computer rooms in six, extremely poor communities. It provides the means for teachers to instill in their students pride in their rich heritage. The fund continues to provide emergency medical assistance, clothing, hot meals and school supplies to a thousand Quechua children each year.

The schools receive no help from the government or other organizations in Peru.

Your purchase of this book places you in the flow of ayni. All proceeds from this beautiful book, after printing expenses, go directly to the Willka T'ika Children's Fund. In isolated villages, far away from the tourist world, smiles of gratitude from the gentle Quechua children will fill your hearts with love.

If you are fortunate to travel to Peru with a special interest group that stays at Willka T'ika's luxury Guest House, located on the grounds of the Chakra Gardens, you may visit one of the schools sponsored by your donation.

Willka T'ika's private Guest House offers priority accommodation to special interest groups. Advance reservations for all guests are essential. For book purchases, Willka T'ika accommodation, Chakra Garden Flower Essences, or information on the wonderful work dedicated to helping Quechua children, please email info@willkatika.com, or visit www.chakragardens.com or www.willkatika.com.

All U.S.A contributions made to the Willka T'ika Children's Fund non-profit 501(c)(3) corporation are tax deductible to the extent allowed by law.

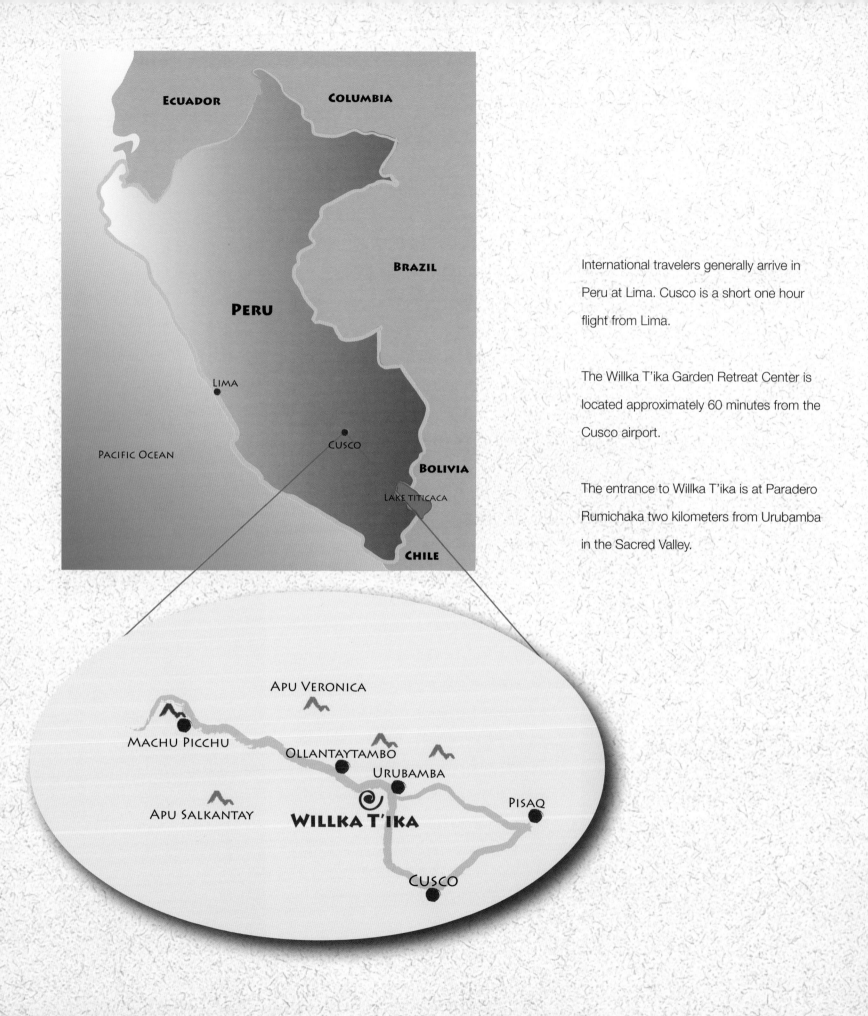

International travelers generally arrive in Peru at Lima. Cusco is a short one hour flight from Lima.

The Willka T'ika Garden Retreat Center is located approximately 60 minutes from the Cusco airport.

The entrance to Willka T'ika is at Paradero Rumichaka two kilometers from Urubamba in the Sacred Valley.

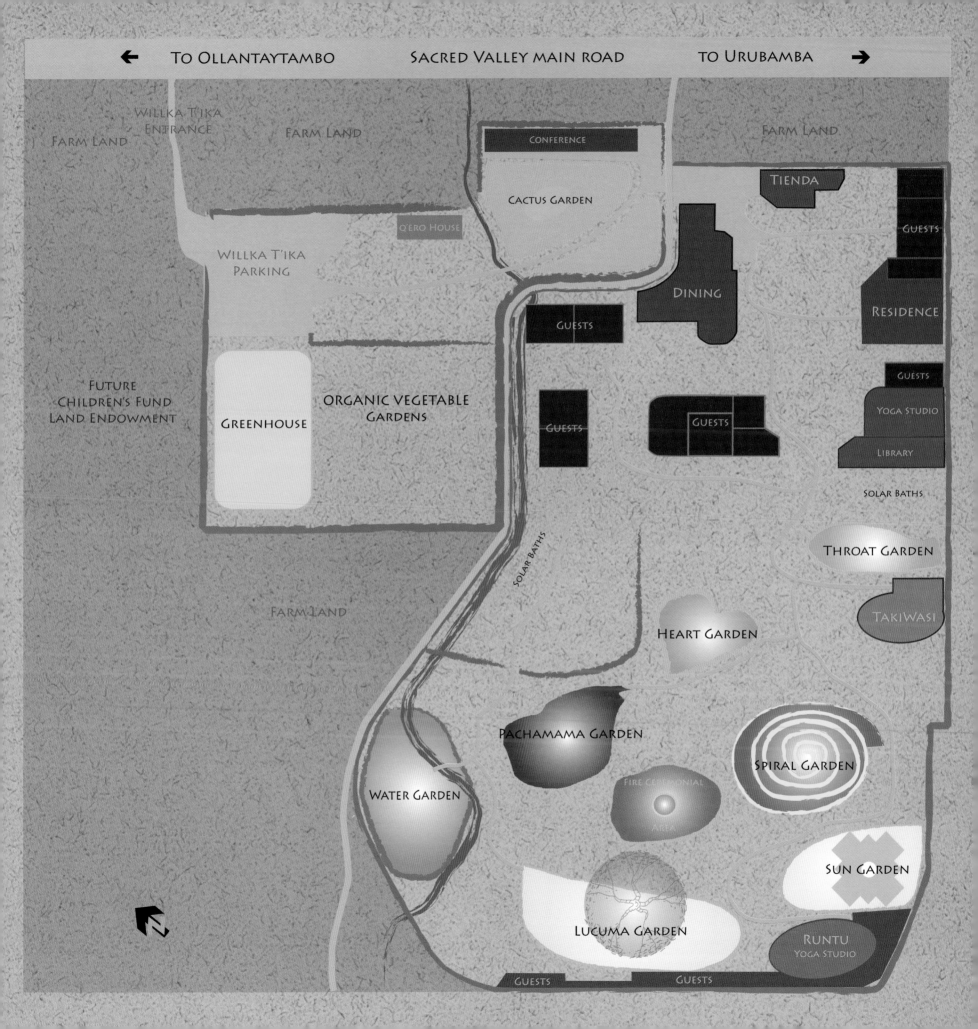

Introduction

Introduction

On a quiet Santa Barbara morning in 1994, I woke up with a strong sense that I must immediately buy land in Peru. After ten years of shamanic visits to its desert, jungle and mountain regions, I had developed a deep connection with the land and people. The Shining Path was no longer a terrorist threat. I knew foreign tourists would soon return in droves. During previous visits, I had looked casually at land for sale, but nothing spoke to me. That day, I scribbled a fax to my Cusco agent saying, "Pachamama (Mother Earth) tells me I must buy land, right now." I knew the exact location and added the words, "in the heart of the Sacred Valley." Within days, I received a fax telling me, "Pachamama has found your land."

You might wonder why I have written a book about chakras, gardening and healing in Peru's Sacred Valley. The short answer is that I have spent more than a decade creating flower-filled, organic gardens which are a model for healing. What began as a home and organic gardens just for me grew into twenty-six guest rooms, two yoga studios, offices, meeting rooms, massage rooms, a library, a music room and a dining room where guests enjoy beautiful organic, vegetarian meals prepared fresh from the gardens.

I became aware that what was happening through me was a synthesis, or joining, of the ancient energy system of the chakras with the Inkan practice of *ayni*.

I wanted to introduce these ideas to the world in an authentic way. Chakras are energy centers that can be felt in the depth of the physical body. Ayni, the ancient practice of exchanging energy, or giving and receiving, needs to be reintroduced to the world. Ayni is in everything. Ayni is life itself. Ayni represents *munay*, pure love.

The ancient Inca built *tampus*, or resting places. These were built for the purification of the body, mind and spirit. In time, my home and gardens were named Willka T'ika, or Sacred Flower, in the Quechua language. They became a modern tampu. Willka T'ika is a resting place away from the busy, commercial world of tourism and crowded, ancient sites. It offers a haven where people can pause to reflect on their lives and spiritual journeys.

Over twelve years, I created seven gardens that corresponded to the chakras of the physical body. The gardens provided a place of rest and healing for me. Subsequently, a number of visitors were drawn to Willka T'ika—first by yoga retreats and later by the incredible gardens that grew from following Nature's guidance. The Quechua, indigenous Andean people, provided information about local

plants, symbols and healing traditions. Their contributions also included building, producing original art and sharing ideas that enhanced the beauty and spirit of Willka T'ika.

After the first four gardens were completed, I realized that Nature had a design for seven sacred gardens. Time spent there in contemplation, meditation and ceremonies helped me find balance and growth. In the gardens I found peace, beauty and miracles. I learned to rejoice in the simplicity of a flower.

The Chakra Gardens at Willka T'ika provide people with a means to expand their consciousness and evolve as spiritual beings. Just as the five physical senses are the gateway through which humans interact with the outer physical world, the seven chakras are the gateway to the inner spiritual world, or the world of the soul. The chakras are the senses of the soul. The soul gives depth, direction and meaning to human lives. Spending time in Nature meditating in chakra gardens expands the awareness of soul. Expanded soul awareness reveals the interconnectedness of all living things. Expanded soul awareness can inspire people to create a healthy relationship with the Earth. It is time for people to open the senses of the soul.

Colors in Nature shape the way we feel and

think. Color vibrations of flowers resonate with the energetic frequencies of chakras. They amplify the senses and stimulate or calm the nervous system. Flower vibrations are known to heal people on the physical and emotional level, bringing love, joy and peace to their souls. I practiced ayni and invited healers to make offerings of gratitude to Pachamama. I observed Nature's ability to transform the body, mind and spirit in an ongoing, everchanging, unending process.

Time passed. I began to feel more strongly the vibrations of flowers which resonated with the chakras of the body. I asked Pachamama and the ancient tree for help. In the process of creating the Chakra Gardens, I learned how taking care of Mother Earth, both giving and receiving, is important for everyone.

One of the great gifts I received in the process of creating the gardens at Willka T'ika is that this information is not limited to my gardens or Peru. These gardens can be recreated by anyone, anywhere, on a scale appropriate for the available space. It is not necessary to use the same plants or symbols I have chosen. By communicating with Nature, people can produce gardens which reflect their own geographical area. They can choose symbols which resonate with them.

If I told you that my journey began with a 1,000-year-old tree which spoke to me, you would probably laugh out loud. The truth is that I found the land, and the lucuma tree called me to create a refuge for healing and restoration. My interaction with the tree was the beginning of a creative partnership with Nature. Planted by the Inkas, the lucuma tree survived in a rocky, barren piece of land. Spontaneously hugging the tree changed my life.

One of the great gifts I received in the process of creating the gardens at Willka T'ika is that this information is not limited to my gardens or Peru. These gardens can be recreated by anyone, anywhere, on a scale appropriate for the available space. It is not necessary to use the same plants or symbols I have chosen...

By sending love and gratitude to Pachamama from individual chakra gardens, we can create a network of energy around the world that contributes to healing our Earth. When groups of like-minded people join to send thoughts of love and appreciation to the planet, it opens new channels to bring light and positive energy back to Pachamama. Pachamama breathes and restores Herself.

Meditating in chakra gardens deeply connects people to Mother Nature and all of Her wisdom. There is an opportunity to receive Universal energy directly. People can learn to trust themselves no matter where they are on their spiritual journeys.

In my journey, I took a leap! I decided to follow my passion when I moved to Peru, leaving behind a marriage, grown children and a comfortable life. I have received many rewards as a result of my decision. I learned from the indigenous people of the Andes. I learned to build without plans or permits, using natural materials. I learned to be an innkeeper. This promoted cross-cultural understanding and brought pleasure to many guests.

Consciously creating chakra gardens provides an effective way to focus Nature's energy in a more personal form. Nature is a grand coordinator of well being. It trains us to become mindful of the Earth and our environment. This book offers a way to support health and wholeness.

In ancient times, people took care of their relationship with Mother Earth. Today, many have forgotten. They take from but do not give back to Pachamama. As people create their chakra gardens, they will move into the world of ayni. As humans move into the practice of ayni, Pachamama will thrive again.

I hope the reader will find understanding and inspiration in reading this book. Finding a personal way to honor and care for Pachamama can restore and balance the Earth. The Andean people have had this understanding for millennia. I want this book to be a reminder of what is possible.

Ultimately, this is a book about love. Love of Nature, love of Nature's gifts and healing abilities. It is about love for Pachamama, our Mother, our Earth. It is about making a commitment to loving, appreciating and healing the Earth and ourselves.

Pachamama

Earth Garden

Pachamama: Earth Garden

Red is the dominant color of Pachamama's garden, replenished with red berries, tiny crimson bugs, bloodshot pebbles and red earthworms working in the ochre soil. The color red, found in Earth's vegetation, has stimulating vibrations that support the energy of the root chakra. Red is a reminder that the courage to clear root chakra blockages is already present within. It is the peace in the scarlet glow of sunset, the passion in the fiery sparks from embers at night. Absorbing the magical, healing properties of flowers and plants in this garden allows red vibrations to fire us up, recharging the body and reactivating life.

Willka T'ika's Earth Garden overflows with red carnations, gladioli, hibiscus, amaranthus, poppies, roses and dancing scarlet fuchsias. They not only share their beauty and exquisite perfumes in the garden, but also make delightful appearances in salads, summer drinks and teas on the dining room tables.

When grouped together, red flowers and plants hold an intense vibration of enthusiasm, creativity and strength. By gazing deeply at the flowers, trees, vines, rocks or soil in this garden, it is possible to sense or visualize spirals of free-flowing, luminous energy. Guests are invited to sit down, take a few deep breaths, close their eyes, and allow Pachamama's vibrations to bring health and harmony to the root chakra.

Red vibrations are energizing and may assist with exhaustion and anemia, acting as a tonic. Red tonics are said to aid colds and chills by getting the circulation going. People who are quick to "see red," or have a flaming temper or high blood pressure, may find it best to "cool their fires" and distance themselves from too much red!

Root chakra: Center of our material and earthly circumstances. Contains the raw, unprocessed kundalini energy used by all chakras.

Meditation symbol: Geometric square. "My needs are met."

Andean garden symbol: Serpent, rocks and vines

Primary color: Red, for courage, confidence and passion

Signature Plant of the Earth Garden

˜Nuqchu

cinta cinta, salvia dombeyi

Crimson clusters of fuchsia-like ñuqchu (nyuj-choo) bloom year round in Pachamama's garden. Cascades of flowers portray abundance, not just material abundance but also love. Their powerful spirit is believed to bring love to the base chakra. Ñuqchu is the signature, or main, plant of the Earth Garden. It represents the energy carried by the garden.

Symbolically, the darker shade in the base of the flowers represents the held energy of an unhappy early life. As the plant grows into masses of beautiful, dainty flowers, it reminds people to let go of a past that no longer serves them, just as the serpent sheds its skin. Ñuqchu's healing energies remind people that transformation into a positive, beautiful and abundant life is possible. For colds and coughs, valley residents steep the flowers in boiled water and drink the infusion three times a day.

Signature Plant of the Earth Garden

Kiwicha

amaranthys candata

In Inkan times, kiwicha, or red amaranthus, was known as a food for the gods. Warriors credited it for their great strength, fearlessness and sexual prowess. It was said to be the color of their blood. It is a strong plant with roots firmly anchored in the earth.

Some believe that while it is growing, its vibrations awaken the third eye, and it imparts a high-pitched, musical sound that stimulates clairaudience and clairvoyance. As it ripens and is consumed, this high-protein cereal offers vital energy thought to aid digestion. Kiwicha is grown throughout the Sacred Valley and sold at all markets.

Red Plants of the Earth Garden

CARNATIONS

Clavel, carnations, especially red ones, are the most favored flower in the Sacred Valley. Pachamama adores their bountiful buds and perfume. Ritual specialists gather the flowers to use in ceremonial offerings to Her. The Andes carry strong mountain energies. When there are seismic shakes and natural movement, it is believed that holding a red clavel, and making an offering to the rivers, will calm and appease the earth. Medicinally, they are used to treat ailments in the base energy center, like kidney and bladder infections. As a tea, clavel petals have a pleasant, lightly perfumed taste. The tea is believed to soothe and calm nervousness and anxiety.

HIBISCUS

Cucarda, red hibiscus flowers, have adapted to the high altitude. As nature's gift to women, they assist in reclaiming and healing their sexuality. Those who desire a satisfying and liberating sexual life can tune into this sexual flower and visualize the flowing warmth surging with joyful passion through the body. There is something playfully erotic about the hibiscus. Undress it and get the juices going! Eat the petals in salads. Have fun with it!

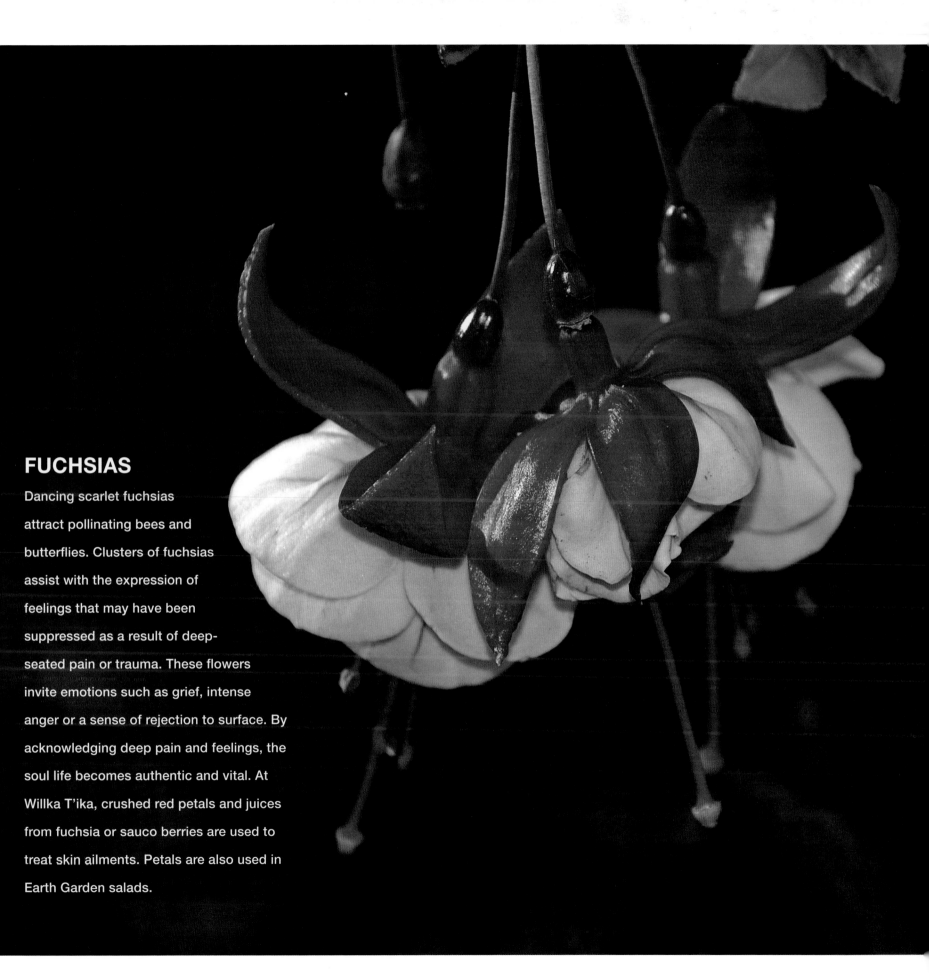

FUCHSIAS

Dancing scarlet fuchsias
attract pollinating bees and
butterflies. Clusters of fuchsias
assist with the expression of
feelings that may have been
suppressed as a result of deep-
seated pain or trauma. These flowers
invite emotions such as grief, intense
anger or a sense of rejection to surface. By
acknowledging deep pain and feelings, the
soul life becomes authentic and vital. At
Willka T'ika, crushed red petals and juices
from fuchsia or sauco berries are used to
treat skin ailments. Petals are also used in
Earth Garden salads.

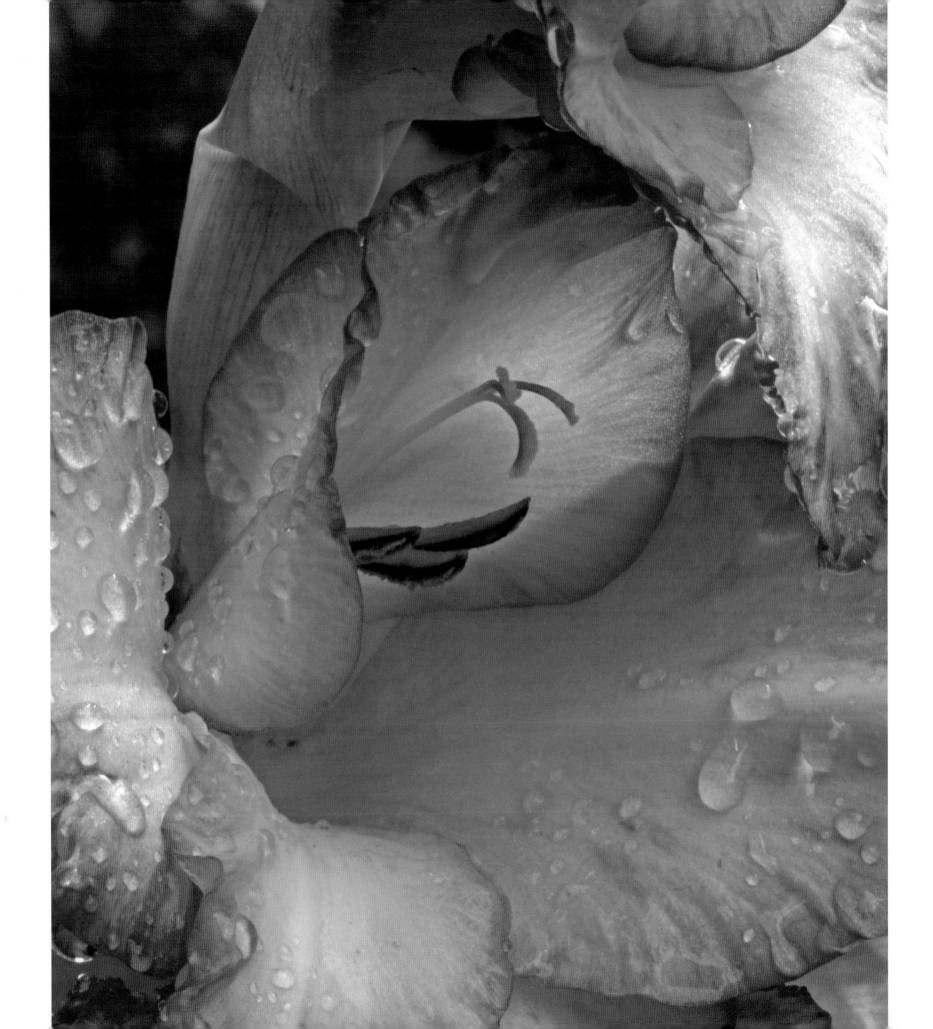

HOLLYHOCKS

(right) The inedible hollyhock, or malva, is an easy-seeder that pops up everywhere. This valley favorite grows year round. Healers recommend using the petals and leaves as a douche to treat cystitis, frequent urination or vaginal problems of the base energy center. When root chakra energy is blocked, parts of red or white hollyhock are used in infusions. It also works as a soothing tonic for coughs, colds and bronchitis. In lotions, the hollyhock soothes skin inflammations and rashes.

GLADIOLI

(left) Upright gladioli stalks filled with beautiful flowers make us "glad" they grow so easily in the Sacred Valley. They are one of the world's most popular cutting flowers, and, when grown organically, the corm can be ground into medicine to treat diarrhea, coughs or colds. Red petals added to salads nourish the base energy center.

ROSES

Nature spirits grow red roses, *rosa roja*, that bloom year round at Willka T'ika. Meditating with a red rose, representing feminine beauty, keeps the heart open--for love is like a red, red rose. Roses, their petals numbering five, or multiples of five, are regarded as sacred. Petals are popular for healing baths, teas, punches and potpourri.

POPPIES

Red poppies, *amapola*, symbolize the blood of those killed in battle. They do not have the potent activity of their relatives, opium poppies. These delicate flowers grow near Willka T'ika's ceremonial fireplace. One moment the beautiful flower is there, and the next, the petals float away and are gone forever. Poppies remind us not to dwell in the past but to enjoy the present moment.

Something about being on the land each day, surrounded by rich, earthy textures, seemed to feed my senses and nourish my soul. Watching the creation of my home, seeing it grow from the dirt while infusing life force back into the earth by replenishing the depleted soil, was such a fulfilling experience.

Creating the Earth Garden

During my first year at Willka T'ika, I hired young Quechua men, children of traditional campesinos (farmers) in the neighborhood, to clear the land of stones and dig up the soil. Happy to find paying work, and eager to tackle what I thought was a formidable task, they arrived promptly to begin work at 7 a.m. each day. After a year clearing stones and digging up the rock-hard soil, only soft, powdery, lifeless clay remained. I instructed the men to plant beans, peas and nitrogen-giving plants, which they tilled back into the ground to feed the earth. All leftover food and plant matter was made into compost then mixed with manure we begged farmers to sell us.

I laughed the first time I bumped into a team of arrieros (muleteers) coming through my property with donkeys, heavily loaded with straw. They had walked four hours from their mountain communities above to deliver straw to be mixed with mud and water to make adobe bricks. After two weeks under the hot, winter sun, the bricks were ready for building. The Inka used the same building method over four hundred years ago. Today, their adobe brick buildings still grace the streets of Cusco.

I ordered more donkey loads of straw for the gardens, and that too was mixed with compost and soil to serve as mulch to protect seedlings from the harsh sun.

Something about being on the land each day, surrounded by rich, earthy textures, seemed to feed my senses and nourish my soul. Watching the creation of my home, seeing it grow from the dirt while infusing life force back into the earth by replenishing the depleted soil, was such a fulfilling experience.

Tucked away in a lower corner of the land, a few old kapuli (small, Andean cherry trees) grew out of the base of old stone walls that separated my land from the neighbor's. As I left for Cusco one morning, I pointed to that section, asking the men to remove the larger stones and prepare the soil for planting. Upon my return, Zorro, the spokesman for the group, sheepishly greeted me with "Señora, we have built you a trono." The entire team stopped working to watch my reaction as I approached the garden. At some point during the day, they decided I needed a throne. Instead of moving the stones away, they arranged and cemented

them into what they considered a comfortable throne. Since it was the first throne I had ever received, I politely thanked them for their special gift and sat there for the longest time wondering what "on earth" I was going to do with it.

Having bonded with my throne, I announced to the men it was definitely serpent-shaped. Relieved that I liked their creative endeavors, they all nodded their heads in agreement. We painted a long, red serpent along the permanent base of the throne.

Each time I returned to sit on my throne, I observed interesting features in the surrounding area. Huge boulders lay together as if they were cave entrances into the earth. Embedded in the boulders, thick, old, woody vines twirled into and out of the kapuli trees. Above the trees in early summer, a tumba (native vine) displayed attractive, inverted, red trumpet flowers that would soon morph into exotic fruits. Birds always beat me to the ripe fruit growing out of my reach and into the sky. Still, I was delighted to welcome a variety of fruit-loving birds onto the grounds.

Summer brought tiny, but delicious, red cherries from the kapuli, attracting even more birds to the throne garden. Beaks filled with fruit, these colorful little birds hopped over to drink from a nearby furrow flowing with fresh water from mountain streams above. Tiny grasses, horsehair, and zapatias (lady's slippers) growing beside the water captured my attention. The seed for a future water garden was planted.

After the rains, cuttings of native shrubs were kindly brought by the Quechua and planted in a sunny section around the throne. These native plants grew quickly, producing ñujchu (crimson clusters of wild fuchsias) that bloom throughout the Andean year. I welcomed the enthusiasm of the young Quechua farmers, eager to share their plant knowledge with me. Thanks to their throne, and my desire to sit upon it, I was joyfully experiencing a garden coming alive with bees, butterflies, insects and birds to interact with the wildflowers and fruits.

Movement and a life force danced around me as I began to feel the energies of the earth humming beneath my feet. With my eyes closed in meditation, everything, even my painted red serpent, appeared to be interacting with unseen energies around the throne. I knew this was exactly where the root chakra garden was supposed to be. I dedicated it to Pachamama.

Emotions from my early childhood surfaced during those early visits to Pachamama's garden. Feeling secure in Her embrace, I was able to acknowledge and feel those emotions. When I felt ready, I would release them to Pachamama. She was happy to receive the energies I no longer required, transmuting them and revealing new growth. Just as the snake sheds its skin, I felt comfortable shedding my past over and over again in Pachamama's Earth Garden.

The spirit of ayni is the reciprocal exchange of living energy that occurs through giving offerings and receiving from Mother Earth.

Andean Lore and the Earth Garden

Representing our passage to full consciousness, *Amaru* (the Inkan serpent) stirs to energize the base energy center of the body. Amaru is associated with inner wisdom, awakening hidden knowledge about life experiences. Its kundalini energy moves from the earth to fuel all the other chakras, bringing enlightenment.

Visualizing ourselves as Amaru—stirring in the inner earth, making its way toward light, constantly renewing itself by moving forward and shedding its skin—is a metaphor for progression through various stages of consciousness. Sloughing off old dogmas and outdated beliefs can reveal fresh lessons and sparkling ideas.

The Andean people have recognized and honored this movement of energy for thousands of years. Traditional Quechua campesinos acknowledge it by making offerings to Mother Earth called haywarikuy, which means "let us play." The Quechua graciously exchange gifts and playful healing energies with their beloved Mother Earth in a delightful ceremony. Central to all Andean ceremonies, the offering consists of a paper "plate" filled with the finest foods and minerals of the earth. As Pachamama receives these offerings, She receives their vibrations of abundance, appreciation and love.

The spirit of ayni is the reciprocal exchange of living energy that occurs through giving offerings and receiving from Mother Earth. Pachamama nourishes the earth so that the people of kaypacha (the world of humans, animals and plants) can thrive in perfect balance. Andean healers, known as pakkos, conduct these ceremonies to Pachamama, assuring health and well being to the senders, their families and their entire community, as well as to the surrounding apukuna (mountain deities) and all of Nature. Practiced in Andean mountain communities, the concept of ayni reinforces the wisdom that man benefits from helping others. Nothing remains static in the Universe where the energies of the physical body are constantly exchanged with those of Pachamama. In order to remain in a state of joy, health, and wealth, one must practice ayni. From a very young age, Andean people learn to give to Pachamama first in order to receive from Her. With a lifestyle that keeps them close to the earth, the Quechua-speaking people understand that all living beings are connected, that everyone comes from Pachamama, breathes Her air, eats Her foods and lives on Her land. People take care of Her animals, which feed and clothe them. Her resources sustain the ongoing cycle of life. Shamans, sages, nature lovers, and now scientists and politicians, are urging people to live in balance with the earth, just as traditional communities have done for centuries.

Variegated red shrubs, scarlet-hued grasses and blushing flowers line the paths leading to the Earth Garden at Willka T'ika. Rope-like vines wind around a giant boulder. The garden invites guests to sit upon a stone throne, home to the serpent of wisdom, or recline on a soft, grassy patch that cushions fertile beds of ochre soil. Rekindling an awareness of wholeness can begin in the garden dedicated to Pachamama, Mother Earth, a sacred living organism filled with fiery, healing energies. The Earth Garden resonates with the body's root chakra.

The Earth Garden's Root Chakra

If the roots aren't deep, the tree can't stand the weather.

--Yogi Bhajan

According to yogic traditions, the root chakra is situated at the base of the spine in the region of the pelvis and sexual organs. The slow rate of vibrations in the root chakra connects people to the earth. Staying rooted, or grounded, is an important way to keep body, mind, and soul balanced on the journey through life.

All life comes from the earth. Earth's nutrients and subtle energies are absorbed by the root chakra. They then travel upward to fuel the other chakras. Being disconnected from the earth and receiving only surface nourishment can cause loss of security and stability. Feeling disconnected, people often turn to outer material life for support and sexual nurturing. This outward focus can overshadow creative instincts and a passion for life.

The root chakra is the source of primal energy, referred to in eastern religions as kundalini or shakti. This is survival energy, requiring that earthly needs for food, shelter, clothing, money and financial order be met. The root chakra directs the adrenal glands to create the fight or flight response essential for physical and emotional survival. This center provides the energy to galvanize people into action when necessary and to manifest their full potential.

Along with survival patterns, early childhood experiences are stored in the root chakra. If nurturing family relationships are experienced, and a stable social group is provided, a strong foundation of emotional security is built. This contributes to a positive perception of life. On the other hand, if emotional trauma or sexual abuse are imprinted in the body, they may create a negative outlook on life. Blockages, or scars relating to abuse, need to be cleared from the earth energy center. The "Contemplation" and "Ceremony" sections at the end of this chapter can assist with clearing blocked root chakra energy.

Power of the Earth Garden

Cultures demonstrate blocked root chakra energies when they cling to the petty differences of their ancient traditions and religious beliefs. Stopped in the energy of fear and survival, the earth energy has not been raised through the other chakras. When regenerative healing forces are held back in the root chakra, they can cause chaos and disease.

Whether living simple lives around the world or sophisticated lives in western countries, people inherently dream about a life in balance. Pachamama nurtures and unifies all forms of life. She can be counted on to provide energy, the life force, we need. Chakra gardens offer a simple, effective way to harmonize an individual's energies with those of the Earth. Continuing to honor and appreciate Her in our daily lives strengthens unity with Nature.

One visitor to Willka T'ika, Marthie, describes her experience of transformation in the Earth Garden:

"My husband died. I had taken some leave to stay at home solely to grieve over Derik. I had consciously wanted to nurture myself. A traveling companion wrapped her bright red pashmina shawl around me. I needed to find out if there was enough energy and emotional strength in me to live fully once more, not just survive. While contemplating in Pachamama's Earth Garden, I realized that our love never disappears. I realized it was never a choice between memories of Derik and a new life. I could have both. I wept deeply for the last time, but these were tears of joy."

"Red is the color of life. It is a color of strength, vitality, joy, energy, passion and love. It is the color of the here and now, the color of survival. Being wrapped in the red of Pachamama's garden helped me move into my new life."

Contemplation

Imagine living in a world where everyone believes and practices the following:

❀ *"My root chakra is open and balanced."*

❀ *"I honor, respect and am deeply connected to Pachamama."*

❀ *"I am connected to Source."*

Release Body Blockages in the Earth Garden

Many guests at Willka T'ika have found the following exercise very valuable for releasing blockages in the body. Some experience pain leaving them. Others feel sick or have diarrhea temporarily; then it passes. People may think this is related to food eaten, but it is, in fact, a cleansing to allow new energies to enter.

Remove your shoes and sit or lie on the rocks or grass in the Earth Garden. Place your hands on the Earth. With closed eyes, breathe quietly. Begin to sense the rhythm of Pachamama, the steady beat of Nature, until it pulsates within your own heart. Become aware of the rich smell of the earth beneath you.

Affirm:

"Pachamama is happy to receive whatever I choose to release. What I release leaves the body and is absorbed by the Earth. I feel the body filling with pure, clean energy coming from the cool, soft, deep earth."

You may want to place soil in the palms of your hands and gaze into it. Pour out all your problems, in minute detail, into the soil. When you are ready, toss the soil away.

Geometric Square

The geometric square represents balance and connection to the four corners of the Earth. Visualize the geometric square on the root chakra of your body.

As you visualize the shape, affirm "My needs are met," until you feel the truth of the statement in your body. This is a simple, powerful reminder that you are secure. You need not fear anything. All your needs are met. Whenever your thoughts return to concern about the future, repeat again, "My needs are met." You can add to that, "My needs are met, always." Feel the energy coming from Pachamama up through your legs into the root chakra, to give you support. Practice visualizing the geometric square on your root chakra whenever you feel the need to reassure yourself that all is well.

I have personally found this very useful during the past sixteen years. Whenever my thoughts would wander to concerns about my security, future, money, I would calmly see the square on my root chakra and say to myself, "My needs are met." It has worked for me. My needs always have been met. They will continue to be met!

New Patterns of Thinking and Feeling

Energy blockages in the root chakra may show up as restrictive patterns that prevent full Self-expression. Placing attention on a new thought pattern, and feeling as if the change already exists, brings it into physical form. Here are some old root chakra patterns and new thought patterns for contemplation.

OLD CHAKRA PATTERN	NEW THOUGHT PATTERNS
• Belief in duality	• I am connected to Divine Source.
• Survival	• I know Spirit provides for all my needs.
• Doubt, fear	• I release my doubt and fear to Pachamama.
• Struggle	• I choose to go with the flow of life.
• Lack of choice	• I define my own life events.
• Inherited ancestral beliefs	• I am free to choose the values I want.
• Financial stress	• My needs are met.

Coca Leaf Offering (Kuka K'intu)

In the Andes, the most precious gift to Pachamama is the coca leaf, mama coca. Pakkos, or healers, work with a k'intu (collection of three leaves) to connect to the three Andean worlds said to make up the totality of cosmology or divine existence. At Willka T'ika, coca leaves are placed into baskets for your use and the following ceremony is suggested. In other locations, different symbolic leaves can be used. Each time you spend time in a chakra garden, you may prepare your own k'intu to offer Mother Earth. Before beginning personal work or meditation in any of the chakra gardens, or before visiting a sacred site, it is customary to show respect or gratitude to Pachamama by offering Her a k'intu.

You are asking Pachamama for what you want. In ayni, the reciprocal exchange of energy, She will bring you what you ask for. You are connecting with the Andean deities, reaffirming your intention and expressing gratitude for what you have received and are about to receive.

Traditional Method

1. Select three coca leaves of the best quality. Arrange them with the dark-green side facing up.

2. Hold the three leaves, at their base, facing up, between your thumb and first finger.

3. Take a few moments to focus on what you are grateful for and what you desire for yourself and others.

4. Place your intent in one leaf for your own wellbeing, in the second leaf for your loved ones and family, in the third leaf for Pachamama, our planet Earth.

5. When ready, without letting the leaves go, blow your essence into the k'intu three times. This is called phukuy. This act sends off your intention to Pachamama and connects your energy to that of the Universe.

6. At any time, you may bury three leaves in the garden of your choice.

Yakuñawi:

Water Garden

Sacral chakra: Center of human emotions focused on creativity, sensuality and sexuality.

Meditation symbol: Qero (goblet). "My desires are fulfilled."

Andean garden symbol: Pujyu (sacred springs) and pajcha (fountains).

Primary color: Orange, for creativity and sexuality.

Yakuñawi: Water Garden

The universe in its most fundamental form is a vast liquid flow of energies swirling in a literal sea of vibrations and currents. In the earthbound world of perception, its metaphorical equivalent is water. Filled with the force of life, precious water moves and changes while nourishing everything on Earth. Flowing throughout the physical body, water keeps it alive, active and healthy. Resonating with the second, or sacral, energy center of the body, *Yakuñawi* (water spring) is the chakra garden that honors water.

The core essence of the water garden and the sacral chakra is creativity. The color orange inspires the beginning of creative projects and encourages participation in social activities involving family or friends.

At Willka T'ika, freshly-harvested organic vegetables such as carrots, peppers and lisa are grated into delicious and nutritious soups. Found in the Andes, lisa is an orange, potato-like bulb. Orange calendula and nasturtium petals, papaya, oranges and mangoes all find their way to Willka T'ika's food tables.

wall panel frescoes by Mario Jannco

Signature Plant of the Water Garden

Andean Sabila

Sabila, or Peruvian aloe vera, is one of the most highly valued, healing plants in the Sacred Valley. For that reason, it is the signature, or main, plant in the Water Garden. Juicy orange flowers resonate with the spirit and soul of water.

Loaded with vitamins, calcium, enzymes and amino acids, this power plant is believed to regenerate cells. The Quechua offer it to guests for skin ailments, burns, bites and stings. They scorch a leaf on a wood fire and apply the hot, succulent flesh to the wound.

Sabila is said to re-infuse the vital force of those who neglect their physical or emotional needs. It is believed the flowing water aspect of the plant cleanses people of unwanted energies and neutralizes the negative vibrations of those who pass by the plants. Andean lore says the skin should not be thrown away after use but buried in the same place it grows.

Orange Plants of the Water Garden

Bold, orange-hued flowers of succulent, healing plants summon us into this garden where the energy emanating from the flowers and blessed waters connect us with the life force of all living things. The rejuvenating vibrations of the color orange express vitality. They swirl around nasturtiums, orange calendula, aloe vera, California poppies, corn of gold and shrubs filled with marmalade-colored flowers. Visiting insects, birds, as well as orange tinged minerals and pebbles added to the garden support the energies, infusing the garden with enthusiasm

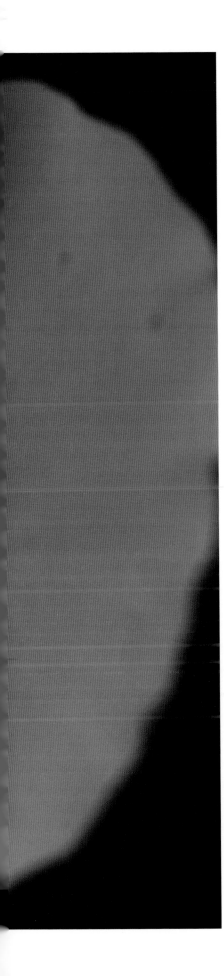

CALIFORNIA POPPY

The light seeds of the orange California poppy scatter in the Andean wind. Blooming in different sections of the garden, dazzling orange flowers delight guests. Though this flower is not used locally as a medicinal herb, its vibrations remind visitors to stop searching for something outside themselves. It encourages taking individual responsibility for being the powerful creator of life rather than giving personal power away to others. The California poppy calls each person to create the strong inner life that is critical to the balance of the sacral energy center. Its message is "The golden light you seek is to be found within yourself."

CALENDULA

The Latin root word, *calenda,* means "first day of the month." Easy to grow, calendulas bloom every month, year round, on Willka T'ika's calendar! Known as a magnificent herb, the calendula has antiseptic, antibacterial, antifungal and astringent properties. If that is not enough, it is said to detoxify the body and soothe skin inflammations. Willka T'ika's cooks throw petals into quinoa and rice dishes, green salads and fruit salads. They bake them into cookies and cakes to be eaten while sipping calendula tea.

To make calendula tea, pour a cup of boiling water over ¼ cup of fresh petals. Steep for five minutes, strain and sip. Cooled and served with a slice or two of fresh orange, it makes a refreshing drink.

Brilliant orange and golden varieties of calendula impart energies that open receptivity to Nature's whisperings of messages beyond words. Vibrationally, these flowers assist with communicating creative potential at a soul level and guiding use of the spoken word in a warm, calm fashion.

NASTURTIUM

Mastuerzo is the Spanish name for nasturtiums. The Quechua gardeners call them uno-uno. I brought these seeds to Willka T'ika, planting them "one-by-one" to decorate the stone walls. At first the plant resisted, but we persisted and threw ash and words of encouragement over their leaves. After two years, nasturtiums decided to join the thriving masses of flowers. Now they self-seed and pop up in areas of their choice. For little effort, uno-uno gives much pleasure. Highly visible and pretty, this natural antibiotic is high in vitamin C and minerals. The Inka incorporated the flowers and seeds into their daily diet. Nasturtiums are said to heal wounds, bring down fevers, banish colds, flu, sore throats and bronchitis. In salads, the silky smooth, orange petals are gorgeous. Buds, leaves and seeds are pickled in vinegar and eaten with grains.

CORN OF GOLD

Choclo de oro (corn of gold) from the Kniphofia family grace our water garden. Choclo refers to sacred corn worshipped during Inkan times. Deep orange-coral, corn-shaped flowers tinged with yellow act as intermediaries between the earth, water and sun chakra gardens. Out of well-drained earth, they grow in full sun and need ample moisture to survive. In the sacral chakra garden, these striking, clump-forming flowers remind guests of their own sacredness. This plant reminds us to stay in balance. All these natural elements are equally important.

Creating the Water Garden

During the rainy season in the Andes, black clouds shroud the 20,000-foot peaks with stormy darkness. To command respect and remind farmers of their awesome power, Andean gods roar with thunder and fill the skies with electrifying flashes of lightning. Sacred waters gush from mighty glaciers above to the farmlands below.

During the Andean dry season at dawn, *Inti* (the sun) illuminates the majestic, silent peaks. Throughout the day, fiery rays beat down upon the plants, scorching their tender growth. Small streams flow down the mountains. To survive, subsistence farmers must pray for water, the most precious commodity on planet Earth.

After living in Peru for some time, I became aware of the need for water to maintain our delicate flower, herb and vegetable gardens year round. I asked the workers to build two, giant, underground water storage tanks for the dry months.

Before moving to Peru, I had a Cusco engineer and two architects design my house. They showed a small, round, plastic septic tank in the garden and a cement-block water tank next to the house in the ground. I knew that both tanks would soon be inadequate. I turned to Mark Hennessy, my partner, for a better idea. He presented me with two professional plans from South Africa. One was for a huge, underground water tank, and the other, a giant septic tank with a French drain that would allow

water to percolate back into the earth. Mark's waving hands, interspersed with incoherent Spanish words, guided local builders during construction as they dug deep and wide into the rocky earth. We used steel bars to reinforce the cement walls forming the underground

septic tank. I could tell the curious builders wondered why this señora was spending so much money on structures no one would ever live in or see. I realized I could not expect my children or friends in the United States to share my excitement over building a "real" septic tank in Peru. All I could do was express gratitude to Mark for introducing the concept to my Quechua neighbors and smile when they adapted the construction plans to their own homes.

In growing communities in the Rumichaka farming area of the Sacred Valley, reservoirs or storage tanks remain luxury items for Quechua farmers who simply rely on rain, ritual and mountain streams to irrigate their crops.

Farmers participate in communal *faenas* (work cooperatives). Members pay a fee and are allotted time slots to receive the flow of mountain water diverted along *sequias* (furrows) to the farmland below. Each member is obligated to donate a few days of work several times a year to ensure

the furrows are maintained. Willka T'ika's Quechua gardeners participate at local water-board meetings.

At 4 a.m. once each week, one of the gardeners walks up the valley to adjust giant keys that divert the water coming down the mountain to our property. As the water gushes in, the Quechua using picks and shovels, carefully guide the flow to flood the gardens. For hundreds of years, Andean farmers have used this method. Deep watering allows us to grow flowers and vegetables year round.

Throughout the Sacred Valley, Andean farmers plant vegetables in rows. Expecting me to plant corn and lettuce, they looked surprised when I announced I would plant flowers. I planted flower seedlings massed together without considering how the wide beds would be watered.

Unable to dig deeply into the hard earth, I called upon ever-smiling Livio. He was quick to learn how to plant flowers in a zigzag formation. Laughing every time I repeated the zigzag mantra, and pointing to a spot in the dirt, he furiously dug a hole with a pick, mixed in compost, and together we planted each precious plant before moving on to the next.

Thanks to the force of gravity, the flooding method reached our unusually-placed gardens.

It proved to be far more efficient than using the fancy sprinkler heads and watering devices I purchased in the United States. Sprinklers and hoses are used only when we need to supplement the watering of delicate plants. We refill our tanks at night, capturing water from the sequias before it runs into the nearby Urubamba River.

We were ready for guests in our third year. It was important for me to use natural resources, so I arranged for a Cusco plumber to make and install solar tanks and panels for our guest bathrooms. Plentiful sun supplied hot water. I wanted to build natural stone outdoor baths for guests to relax under the southern stars, so I ordered additional solar tanks. I brought in local stonemasons to carve the baths and work on a water feature. We ordered tons of large boulders from a quarry, miles up a valley. After laboriously hauling in the boulders and dragging them along the path to our property, workers began the project. For the water feature workers were inspired by the Inkan fountains of Tampumachay, gateway to the holy city of Cusco. During the next six months, all day long, you could hear the "tik-tik" of the men hand-chipping the stone.

They completed their magnificent work, a tremendous labor of love and pride. I had no doubt that the huge Inkan wall with niches and

fountains was built to honor *yaku*, the precious water element. The natural, flowing stream running beside the water garden bestowed a soothing energy.

The human body is largely made up of water, as is the earth's physical structure. Water carries vibrations and is capable of sensing and receiving positive and negative frequencies that pass through it. As it circulates the planet, water faithfully mirrors all the vibrations created in the world, whether good or bad.

In Masaru Emoto's book, *The Hidden Messages in Water,* he cites research showing that the crystalline structure of water is affected by emotions, thoughts and words. Humans affect and contribute to the state of the world they live in. A garden dedicated to honor water is a reminder to continue to focus on dispersing the purifying vibrations of love, peace and gratitude into water.

I looked forward to meditating in the water garden. I repeatedly sent positive thoughts to the water gracing our land by calling upon *Yakumama* (Mother Spirit of Water). I visualized water vapor carrying positive vibrations to the highest Andean peaks. From there, purified rains returned to keep the world of plants, humans and animals alive. Together with all living beings and plants, I became part of this circle of life energy. I felt the flowing vibrations

of water align with the energies of my sacral chakra. I found this garden a wonderful place to disperse positive vibrations through Willka T'ika's garden water as it prepared to join the sacred Urubamba River then flow into the immense Amazon River and to the sea as an integral part of all Mother Earth's water.

The soft sounds of running water invited me to pause in Yakuñawi. While I was sitting on a rock facing *pajcha*, or fountains, emotions swirled within my body. I felt as if I were swimming in a river of water energies flowing within and around me. Creative ideas flourished. Opening my eyes, I became aware of the warm embrace of the sun's rays upon my back. Life would not exist without the energy of the sun warming the earth. Water makes the Earth productive. Without it, Pachamama is dry and desiccated. In order for the combination of water and earth to bring forth life, the energy of the Sun has to be included.

The Sun's energy in my solar plexus empowered me to act. It would bring the full potential of my ideas and emotions into real life. This allowed me to be productive and fulfilled. I accepted Nature's invitation to create a Sun Garden of light, warmth and action.

"Where there is water, there is life." Always venerated in the Andes, water was understood by the Inka as a vital element needed to support life. Myths concerning water explained the origins of life and the world. All sources of water were regarded as sacred. Springs were revered as entrances to *ukhupacha* (inner earth). Waters coming from the sacred mountains were believed to take on the powers of their Source. To honor water, *pakkokuna* (shamans) conducted ritual purification ceremonies in their temples and mountain sites to the Mother Spirit of Water. "*Yakumama, Yakumama,*" they whisper today in rituals to invoke Her spirit.

Andean Lore and the Water Garden

Stone water temples represent the three worlds of Andean cosmology: *Hanakpacha,* (upper world of divinity), *kaypacha* (world of humans, plants and animals) and *ukhupacha* (the world within) symbolize the interconnection of all planes of existence, and the beings, both seen and unseen, that inhabit each world.

The Inka understood the purifying forces of water coming from the high mountain gods and worshipped the water as it journeyed into the Urubamba, formerly known as the Willkamayu. To the Inka, this was a sacred river that fed into and connected with the immense Amazon River basin. It then circulated through the solar system as the *ch'askamayu* (river of stars or Milky Way) before returning to the earth on a never-ending journey.

Willka means "sacred" in the Quechua language. Over and over again the Inka used the word to pay homage to their sacred flowers (*Willka T'ikakuna*) and the sacred river (*Willkamayu*) flowing through the magnificent Sacred Valley (*Willka Bamba*).

These Quechua-speaking people, whose language consists of sounds that mimic and carry the pure vibrations of Nature, understood the flow of life and the energetic connection of all things. Among the original ecologists and environmentalists on the continent, the Inka were superb architects and technological geniuses.

The Inka brought long-term prosperity to an entire empire by being aware of the environmental impact of their farming, and using organic farming practices and conservation techniques,. Building irrigation systems throughout their land, the Inka used stone canals to carry water from sacred glaciers through the mountains to agricultural fields in the valleys below. Stone altars, showing deep appreciation to Pachamama for Her water, dotted the landscape.

(*opposite*) The Sacred Valley and the Willkamayu River from the ruins of the Inka city of Pisac. *(right)* The sacred water entrance to Uhkupacha at the recently excavated Inkan temple of Poqen K'anchay near Willka T'ika

The Water Garden's Sacral Chakra

Life force implies an ebb and flow of energies moving and shifting. The sacral chakra, located below the navel in the lower abdomen, is the center of emotions, representing the flow of life. Creativity, sensuality and sexuality are examples of emotional energies that flow within humans.

The interchange of flowing energies between ourselves and Nature can be felt in the soothing water garden. The basic energies in the root chakra nourish the soul and fill humans with passion and sexual pleasure. The second, or sacral, chakra resonates with the vibrations of water. It provides a window into the unconscious realm where deep-seated, hidden attitudes about self are found. Emotions reveal how humans truly view, value and honor themselves. This energy center draws attention to emotions that should be addressed or healed. The way people deal with their emotions affects their overall physical health.

In addition to being the source of pleasurable sensual and sexual feelings, the sacral chakra is the source of material pleasure. Beliefs about worthiness, or deserving abundance, stem from this center. People who were brought up to love themselves are less likely to have issues with sex or money. A healthy attitude toward

money relates to the idea of fluidity in life. To prevent stagnation, water must keep flowing. The same applies to money, which is referred to as "currency". Money needs to flow like a current in order to function optimally. In financial terms, people talk of being liquid, which refers to having money that is ready to flow. Affluence, or abundance, comes from the root word

affluere, which means to flow. When any flow is blocked, it results in weakened energy. In the sacral chakra, this leads to emotional problems. Notice how you speak about money to others. Is it always about lack, or is it about joining the endless flow of life?

Those who are unaware emotions come from within may find themselves on an endless external search for the meaning of life. Observing yourself looking outwardly to satisfy needs is a sign the flow of energy in the sacral chakra is blocked. Physically, people may suffer from indigestion, sexual or reproductive disorders. Blockages in the sacral chakra often appear as problems with the kidneys or spleen.

A desire for change must include a willingness to change thoughts.

People are born with a natural flow of creative energy. Life experiences can pollute, block or divert that energy into negative attitudes and behaviors. Some of these experiences are lack of parental attention, broken families, religious dogma and sexual abuse. Blockages in the sacral chakra can prevent people from living a truly creative life.

At the global level, blockages in sacral chakra energy can be observed when the free flow of ideas between cultures and people is prohibited. People lose touch with their inherent goodness, common purpose and shared values.

The innate creativity of the Quechua-speaking people was suppressed for hundreds of years after the Spanish conquered the Inka. Sacral chakra energy remained blocked. In the last century, as foreigners began to visit Machu Picchu and purchase goods, colorful crafts began to flourish again. Andinos have become more comfortable with the idea that their traditions and beliefs, suppressed for so long, are of interest to and valued by people from other parts of the world. Spontaneous creativity is beginning to reappear. Sacral energy is beginning to flow once again. Attempts are being made to encourage communities to preserve and expand their ancient, artistic textile skills.

Power of the Water Garden

The most precious commodity on the planet today is water. World-wide contamination and neglect of rivers and water supplies require the full attention and action of mankind. With tourism to Peru on the rise and new hotels appearing in the Sacred Valley, urgent issues relating to water must be addressed.

Through their own efforts, individuals can contribute to the honoring of water. This begins with a conscious effort in your own garden by living and building responsibly and organically. Remaining mindful of the environment and dedicating a garden to yaku, water, helps take care of Pachamama. Her water is required for the survival of all life.

In the pure energies of a water garden, focus on sending love and blessings to honor the Spirit of Water, Yakumama. By doing that, you honor and heal yourself. With a clear intention to send loving thoughts to water, you are able to purify and revitalize this precious and priceless element.

Imagine living in a world where everyone believes and practices the following:

* *"I love, honor and respect water."*

* *"My sacral chakra is open and balanced."*

* *"I am deeply connected to Pachamama's water."*

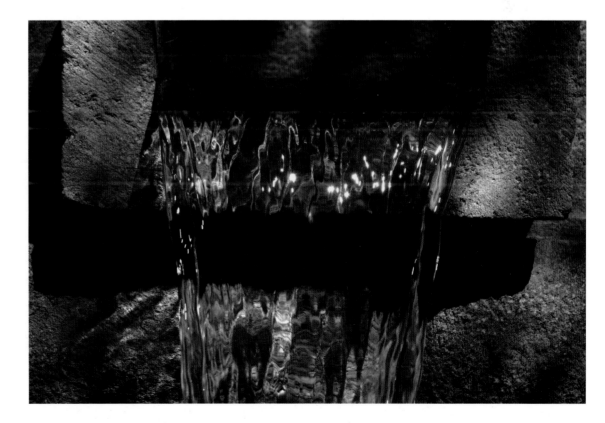

Meditation on the Q'ero

The goblet or q'ero was used in Inkan temple ceremonies. It was filled with *akka*, commonly known today as chicha, a rich alcoholic beverage fermented from corn. *Sara* (sacred corn) was the symbol of abundance and fertility. Filled goblets represented special offerings to Pachamama and the Apukuna, the mountain deities.

Visualize a filled goblet on the sacral chakra of your body. As you visualize the shape, affirm *"My desires are fulfilled,"* until you feel the truth of the statement in your body.

As you ask, so you receive. By meditating on the symbol of the filled goblet in your sacral chakra area, you are reminded that there is no lack. You have all that you desire. It already is in place.

Reflections in a Solar Bath

While the solar baths are not actually located in the Water Garden, they are certainly related to it. Some guests come to Willka T'ika especially for the solar baths. The experience can be recreated in other locations, including your own home, as you dream of being under the river of stars at Willka T'ika.

In this magical setting, beneath *ch'askamayu*, the Milky Way, Nature invites you to submerge your body in steaming water. In this solar bath carved from natural stone and energized by the sun, the hot water is infused with healing vibrations. This water contains the energies of fragrant flowers, medicinal plants and organic salts.

Allow yourself to become fluid, as if flowing in the stream of life. Breathe in and out as you invite these powerful elements to weave healing energies through your body. Let any discomfort flow away with the water. Know that the water allows those discomforts to be recycled by Mother Earth. After your bath continue to take care of yourself. Wrap yourself in a robe before stepping into the cold night air. Drink hot maté (fresh herbal tea). Slip into a cozy bed. As you move into your dreams, the healing energies continue.

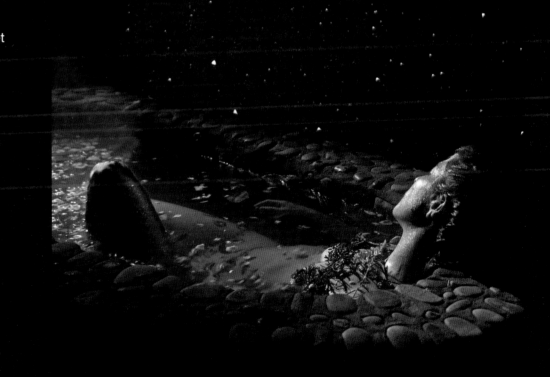

New Patterns of Thinking and Feeling

Energy blockages in the sacral chakra may show up as restrictive patterns that prevent full Self-expression. Placing attention on a new thought pattern, and feeling as if the change already exists, brings it into physical form. Here are some old sacral chakra patterns and new thought patterns for contemplation.

OLD CHAKRA PATTERN	NEW THOUGHT PATTERNS
• Blame	• I am the powerful creator of my life.
• Addictions	• I am fully present. I participate in life freely, joyfully, completely.
• Belief in lack	• My desires are fulfilled.
• Suppressing or ignoring	• I honor my feelings and their emotions or feelings expression.
• Dishonoring or abusing the body	• I love and honor my body. • I feel good about my sexuality.
• Searching outside of Self	• I am worthy of love. • I am whole and complete. • I have a right to express my desires.

Sacral Chakra Healing Ceremony

Water is a wonderful way to clear blocked chakras, especially the energies in the region of the sacral energy center. A focused ritual enables lighter energies to flow via your solar plexus to your heart chakra, so that love, power and wisdom can be brought into all areas of your life.

Approaching a fountain or stream, ask the guardian spirits of the site for permission to be there. Surround yourself with the forces of light. Ask for the healing you would like to receive during the water ritual. Place your hands in your preferred prayer position. Ask to connect with Yakumama. Indicate that you are ready to receive healing.

In your mind, direct the water to the area of your body that needs healing. Place a few drops of water on the crown chakra at the top of your head. Repeat the motion at your third-eye chakra between your eyebrows. Repeat

it again at the throat chakra. Place water on any other chakras you would like to balance by touching. The choice of chakras and the order you do this does not matter. Once you feel your chakras are balanced, visualize energy moving to your water chakra, or sacral energy center. The spirit of water resonates with water everywhere. Use water as a medium to carry messages. Send messages of love and gratitude to your body, to others you love, and to living beings in all dimensions. When you feel complete, thank Yakumama and the water spirits for the healing. Sit in meditation.

Some people may experience temporary discomfort with the physical release of old energies stuck in the body. This may present itself as diarrhea, vomiting or flu-like symptoms. Often this is Nature's way of speeding up the process to release old, unwanted energies and create space for the new. Replenish your body with healing herbal teas.

74 Yakuñawi: Water Garden

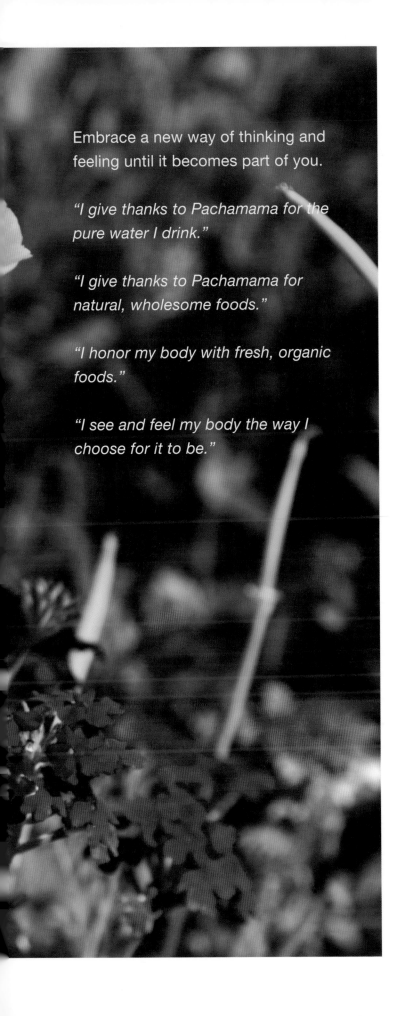

Embrace a new way of thinking and feeling until it becomes part of you.

"I give thanks to Pachamama for the pure water I drink."

"I give thanks to Pachamama for natural, wholesome foods."

"I honor my body with fresh, organic foods."

"I see and feel my body the way I choose for it to be."

Mini-Ceremonies

Place a crystal into a glass or jug of water and set it in the sun. Add a slice of orange and drink it while visualizing the tonic effects.

Drink healing teas of chamomile or lemon grass during late afternoon hours when the gentle orange rays of the setting sun offer soothing qualities.

Place orange-colored stones into a glass of water, and set it in the sun's rays to absorb the energies. Drink the water with awareness and ceremony at night.

Treat yourself to a basket of Andean healing herbs with mineral salts. Add them to bath waters to balance energies and cleanse toxins.

Take a walk in the rain. This is good for both the Earth and Water elements. Laugh, have fun, be sexy, be silly.

Note: It is important to drink two litres of water each day.

Inti:

Sun Garden

Inti: Sun Garden

Nina (the Spirit of Fire) manifests itself as *Inti*, the Sun. Inti holds the essence of passionate, active energy in the Sun Garden. Dazzling yellow flowers, golden butterflies and medicinal herbs dance beneath sunny, blue skies in the garden created to honor the Sun. This lively Sun Garden focuses on the energies of the solar plexus chakra.

Yellow is the color of the sun, source of all living energy. Vibrations emanating from masses of flowers in the Sun Garden lift the energy levels and spirits of guests. This assists them in connecting with the source of their life energy. Working through the solar plexus chakra, yellow is said to assist humans with developing intellectually, physically and emotionally. Energies emanating from sunrays, yellow butterfly wings and golden flower petals bring hope and optimism as well. This helps people assimilate new ideas, contributing to a constructive, fulfilling life.

Solar Plexus Chakra: Center of power and energy for projecting the physical and emotional self into the world.

Meditation symbol: Circle. "I Am."

Andean garden symbol: Chakana (Andean cross), puma (Andean lion), fire element, active light.

Primary color: Yellow to empower, boost confidence and stimulate mental thoughts.

Signature Plant of the Sun Garden

Ruda

A strong, popular and important protection plant, *ruda* grows at all entrances to Willka T'ika. Andean vendors place the fresh, yellow flowers at doorways to attract business and money. Known as rue in the west, it is widely used in the countryside for children in distress. Representing the golden light of life in the solar plexus, ruda is the signature plant of the Sun Garden.

To remove negative energies from the solar plexus, ruda leaves are rubbed together in the hands to extract the potent juices. When the juices are cupped under the nostrils, and the aroma deeply inhaled, the healing effect of this plant can be instantaneous. Ruda, placed on the solar plexus of a reclining person, can help them feel much better within minutes.

Ruda is an all-purpose easy-to-grow herb. Honeybees buzz actively around the masses of tiny, yellow flowers. Ruda gives their honey a pleasantly distinctive taste. Drunk as a mate, or tea, ruda may relieve tension headaches and reduce feelings of anxiety. Since this is not a sweet tasting or smelling herb, use it sparingly in teas. To ease sun-related headaches, a small snip of ruda stem, with leaves and flowers, can be placed on the head under a hat. This practice, in addition to drinking water, is thought to make headaches disappear. Ruda helps newly arrived visitors with altitude-related sickness breathe freely. Guests say it helps them feel grounded.

The fragrance is so strong, even flies and fleas don't like it, making it ideal to grow near roses or hang in kennels and kitchens.

CHRYSANTHEMUM

The joyful spirit of the yellow *crisantimum*, or chrysanthemum, may soothe emotions, dispelling irritation and depression. The vibrations of this bright flower encourage connection with the higher self or Source energy. The energies of the flower remind us to contemplate the impermanent nature of life. Crisantimum is said to be good for eye problems, beauty treatments and the de-wrinkling of skin. For a deep, cleansing facial steam bath, mash crushed yellow petals in honey. If the cook locks her precious honey away in the pantry, take seeds, add them to boiling water, and the effect will be the same.

DANDELION

Western gardeners remove dandelions, or *diente de leon*, as unsightly weeds. Andean farmers leave them wherever they grow for medicinal use when necessary. The flowers encourage listening to physical and emotional needs. The plant is used to reduce bodily and muscular tension. Tensions can be released to flow effortlessly from the body. Tea is prepared from the roots and leaves. Tender, young leaves, full of vitamins and minerals, are eaten in salads. For bodily aches and muscular pain, use diente de leon and never complain.

QUINOA OR QUINUA

When you see plants growing naturally in the gardens, know that it is their intention to be there. Brownish-crimson, self-seeded stalks of flowering quinoa pop up in different areas of the gardens. As the ripening cereal turns golden, the healing vibrations of this plant relate to the solar plexus chakra. High in protein, *quinoa* feeds the body and helps clean the digestive system. Quinoa is believed to assist people with problems in the solar plexus region that may be related to spiritual or emotional imbalance. Muña and Andean kuñuka are also used in teas to assist with digestive problems in the solar plexus area.

RETAMA

A member of the broom family, *retama*, is said to uplift pessimists. Its yellow flowers grow along roadsides in the Sacred Valley. The delightfully fragrant flowers can infuse travelers with positive feelings, providing encouragement. Wonderful in a soothing solar bath, they also are used as a cough remedy.

LADY'S SLIPPERS

Watch your step! In the lush vegetation alongside Willka T'ika's fresh-water stream, tiny *zapatias*, yellow lady's slippers, work hard at grounding guests by assisting with bringing spiritual power into the lower energy centers. Andean healers use the roots to reduce stress, anxiety attacks, emotional tension and nervous pain.

MULLEIN

Tiny buttercup flowers, or *mullein*, twinkle like lights in the sun garden, bloom one after another and are dearly loved by bees. Vibrationally, this tall plant encourages the exploration of psychic and spiritual dimensions. It also encourages clear expression and a sense of integrity. In plant lore, dried mullein leaves were dipped into oil or wax to bring in magical spirits to help people during times of danger. During ceremonies at Willka T'ika, dried leaves are used in incense to purify, and ward away, unwanted energies.

HONEYSUCKLE

Madre de la selva, or honeysuckle, is a hardy creeper that reminds guests to learn from the past and release aspects that no longer serve them so they can fully flourish in the present. This delicate, easy-to-grow flower affectionately entices garden visitors to inhale its delightful fragrance. Edible and easily propagated, this generous plant displays great abundance. Like the best kind of guest, honeysuckle makes no fuss and adapts to any environment.

FENNEL

Enojo, fennel, is a multi-use medicinal herb growing abundantly around the Sun Garden. At Willka T'ika, situated at an altitude of 9,000 feet, many

guests experience what is referred to as "high-altitude flatulence." It can be helpful to drink tea from the leaves of fennel and chew the seeds.

Fennel is used for heartburn, colic, and the digestive system. Delicate leaves have a pleasant, licorice taste. Valley residents chew them for clearer

vision and sweet breath. Chewing the seeds reportedly diminishes hunger pangs and stops stomach rumblings. On a vibrational level, flowers

of enojo help harmonize psychic influences in daily living. Chewing enojo seeds helps people stay awake during long-winded meetings. Enojo is

offered in the herbal tea basket, or guests can chew the leaves directly from the garden plants.

SUNFLOWER

Guests' spirits automatically rise up when they see sunflowers growing in gardens. As the bright, round, golden-colored "faces" follow the Sun, they seem to infuse visitors with joy. *Girasoles*, or sunflowers, which always face the light, encourage speaking truthfully and precise, clear thinking. The sun brings warmth to the soul, assisting with the release of stubbornness and limitations. The seeds make delicious snacks, and, when sprouted, provide a highly nutritious addition to salads.

92 Inti: Sun Garden

Creating the Sun Garden

Growing up in the warm South African climate and living for twenty years in sunny California, I took the sun for granted. When Canadian guests began to stay at Willka T'ika, each afternoon they changed into vests and shorts then gravitated to the area of the garden touched by the last rays of the sun. Hungry for the warmth of the sun, other guests did the same. It was time to create a special garden to honor and appreciate Inti, the Sun God.

It is understandable how this valley became sacred to the Inka. Warm, sunny days were a wonderful contrast to the cold, winter temperatures in the nearby imperial city of Cusco. Inti's giant rays illuminated the Sacred Valley, enabling flowers and vegetables to grow year round.

Sitting in the future Sun Garden, I envisioned a bed of green grass radiating outward in the shape of a giant *chakana*, or Andean cross, a cosmological representation of the three Andean worlds. I saw brilliant gold and yellow flowers surrounding the chakana. The gardeners and I cleared the area until we had

enough space. With chalk and sticks, we had fun calculating the measurements of its square design. The men took wheelbarrows to nearby Pumawanka Valley (place of the puma), to fill them with chunks of *ch'ampa* (thick-growing

grass). The sod was cut from the soil. We watered the newly-planted grass daily. The chakana was filled with a variety of small cuttings from yellow, flowering plants.

One month later, the Sun Garden proudly displayed a golden, flower-filled chakana personifying the glory of the Andean cosmology. On the lawn, a stone puma, or Andean lion, symbolizing power and courage, drew guests into its space. Near the garden, we built *ninawasi* (an indoor structure to honor

fire). In this highly-energized garden, guests could honor and appreciate the Inkan Sun God. The puma, myriad yellow flowers and the Sun's vibrations energized and activated fire energy in the solar-plexus chakra, reminding visitors to reclaim their personal power.

After the visit of a *feng shui* master, the chakana was expanded to allow more sun to enter the garden. Guests could now sit and meditate in its center and receive the healing energies of the early morning sun. Medicinal plants, golden corn and yellow flowers were added. Ruda, a magical, yellow-flowered Andean plant of protection, attracted butterflies, bees and insects. Nature's vibrant forces were absorbed into the solar plexus of those drawn to the garden.

Andean Lore and the Sun Garden

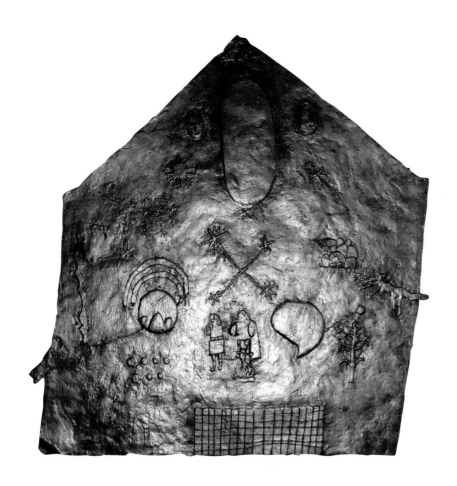

Ancient people understood that without the Sun nothing would grow, and there would be no life. The Inka believed that Inti's energy needed to be mediated and controlled. Inkan temples were built to honor and appease Inti whose tremendous power could accomplish both positive and negative acts. The Sun became the most important symbol of Nature to the Inka. Their temples of gold represented the Sun God.

To appease the Sun God, the Inkakuna (Inka people) lined the temple walls with gold and silver sheets. Rooms were filled with ornaments of the same precious metals. In Cusco, which was built in the shape of a puma, the Inkas built the Q'orikancha which became the model for all Inkan temples. The Sun Garden reflects and represents the importance of the sun in Andean lore.

The Inka capital city of Cusco contained many temples and sacred places including rocks, caves, springs, called *wakas*. The wakas were connected with each other by imaginary energy lines called seqes radiating from Q'orikancha- the great Inkan Sun temple. Seqe lines pass directly through Willka Tika. The gold disk, a replica of the Inkan creation story, is believed to be the most sacred object contained at Q'orikancha.

--seqe lines painting by Miguel Araoz Cartegena

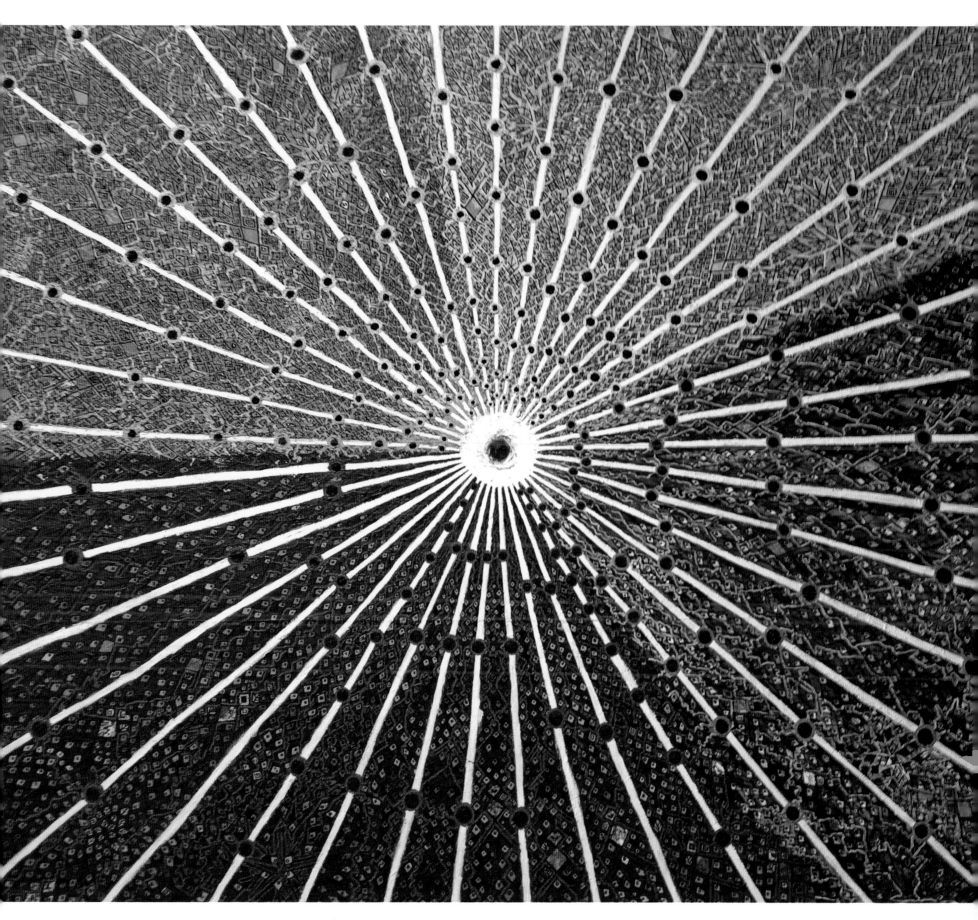

Inti: Sun Garden 95

"If you wish to know the Divine, feel the wind on your face and the warm sun on your hand."   – Gautama Buddha

The Sun Garden's Solar Plexus Chakra

In this chakra, people receive the energy which supports the physical body and the other chakras. The solar plexus energy develops the personal identity that is carried for life. Like the power of the sun, solar plexus energy needs to be balanced. Too much sun will burn tender plants, while too little sun does not support growth. At times it is important for this chakra to be open and active. At other times, such as when one person is actively trying to dominate the thinking or feelings of another, it is important to keep it closed.

This chakra influences the pancreas and affects nutritional absorption. When the solar plexus is blocked, it may create problems within the digestive system.

Many guests come to Willka T'ika with blocked solar plexus energy. This blockage may express as anger and fear. Anger covers a huge realm of emotional experiences. When the world does not appear exactly the way people want it to be, it often triggers anger. It may seem better to become angry than to experience the pain which may lie beneath anger. Expressing anger may provide only a temporary release. Anger or rage is an experience of powerlessness and lack of self worth. When people don't know

how to express anger appropriately, they may be compensating for a lack of inner power and control in their lives. Unexpressed feelings may have physical consequences. Personal power comes from within, not from the external world. A willingness to face unwanted emotions and do the necessary work is part of a commitment to healing.

When people commit to healing themselves and begin to look within to understand their pain, they recognize the causes of anger. A qualified therapist, or participation in anger management, is helpful for people who are aware that they have anger and pain issues.

When I first moved to Peru to build a house and yoga studio, I was faced with many challenges. I mistakenly thought puma power meant that I needed to fight for my rights with local businesses. These were people who conducted business in a completely different way than I did. I soon learned that my approach only resulted in draining my energy. A real puma would not expend energy on anything unessential.

The young Quechua workers at Willka T'ika were my greatest teachers. They taught me to conduct business in a quiet, non-confrontational way. Their methods did not necessarily produce instantaneous results. I learned the importance of recognizing and releasing unpleasant emotions present in my solar plexus. Learning to release negative energies clearly served me over the next decade of my life in Peru.

As Inti connects his energies with humans, they are encouraged to look deeply within to recognize their own Sun power. Dedicated to the Sun's energies, this garden encourages guests to become empowered with a strong and confident sense of self.

Power of the Sun Garden

Inti, the Sun, provides Source energy to produce growth, health and happiness. When focused in any one of the main chakra centers, it produces imbalance. When sun energy is directed only to the chakras above the heart, it can create a "dry" intellectualism, or an "ivory-tower" mentality. When directed only at the chakras below the heart, it can cause misdirected passion and obsession. Blockages in solar plexus energy result in fear, anger and hostility. In the past, the Quechua experienced a narrowing of their solar plexus energies.

They lived in a disempowered manner. At the beginning of this millennium, new agricultural and irrigation programs were initiated in Peruvian desert regions. Businessmen and farmers began to grow *palta* (avocados), mangoes and other exotic fruits. For the first time in decades, Peru entered the world market and is exporting more produce than ever before. Peruvians are waking up to the benefits. Focusing on solar plexus energy, Peruvians have moved into action and are creating prosperity.

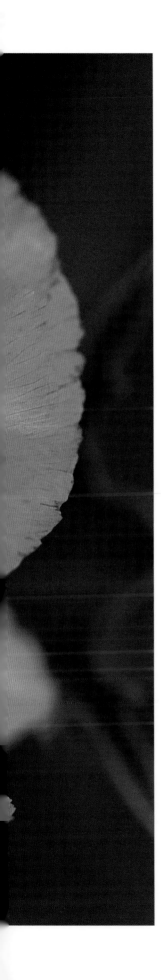

Meditation in the Sun Garden

The meditation symbol of the Sun Garden is a circle, just like the sun itself. When the circle is mentally placed above the solar plexus, it represents the fire elements of Inti, the Sun. Fill your sacral chakra with Sun energies, and feel yourself becoming empowered. Use the affirmation, "I am."

I firmly plant my feet on Pachamama and reach up to Her golden rays.

Here I stand – focused, strong and certain of every word I say.

Forgotten are the thoughts of being unworthy, weak or hopeless.

My inner flame burns bright, even through ink-black nights.

See my light, and feel my fire.

To happiness and openness do I aspire.

~ Juria Maree

Chakana Journey into the Light

Sit comfortably within the grass chakana of the Sun Garden. Close your eyes. Surround yourself with bright light, and breathe the Sun energies into your solar plexus. Feel the energy move to activate all your chakras. When ready, visualize yourself moving on an inner journey through the steps of the chakana. If you see light, follow it. Enter a portal of light, allowing yourself to embark on a transformational journey to expand your energy and light. Each step into the light offers new insights and wisdom. Feel your spiritual awareness expanding and your knowledge increasing. Open yourself up to perspectives of your past, present and future lives. Listen for personal messages. Take the opportunity to reappraise where you are on your spiritual path. Working deeply in the Sun Garden may create a profound, ever-changing realm of experience for you and motivate you to take giant steps into the future. Allow and accept this wisdom from the chakana in the Sun.

A Morning Greeting to Inti

It's simply wonderful to greet the Andean Sun in the early morning hours. Breathe consciously, allowing sunrays to wash over your energy centers. *Prana* (life force) is seen as the energy of life itself in all its forms—physical, emotional, mental, spiritual, evolutional, and, ultimately, transcendental.

- Feel the special energy of sunrays enter the crown chakra at the top of your head. Move this energy into your solar plexus.

- Breathe the earth and water energies into your solar plexus.

- Allow the energies to fuse with the sunlight and ignite into action. Feel the activated energy move through all your chakras and out into the universe.

- Repeat this exercise a few times until you feel charged with the Sun's energy.

- Spend at least twenty minutes in the Sun each day.

- Conscious breathing allows you to absorb vibrations of flowers, plants and vegetables. Vibrations may be experienced as colors, sounds or feelings.

A Practice for Puma Power

Energized by the sun, the puma focuses on what he needs. If he loses his prey while hunting, he does not sit back and bemoan his loss. Still hungry, he moves ahead, focusing on the next animal that comes into his sight. The Andean puma teaches you to stay focused on what you want to attract it into your life.

- Become aware of feelings in the solar plexus region. Simply acknowledge the emotion and any thoughts or feelings that accompany the emotion.

- Calmly release any tension or negative energy. breathe deeply into your solar plexus energy center, then breathe out, let those negative thoughts go.

- It is your choice whether to place a golden shield over your chakras, say nothing, walk away or hold up your palm to send energy right back to the sender. It really is your choice.

- Consciously keep your solar plexus chakra closed during challenging times.

- If you stay focused on someone's anger, rage or pain, you draw more of that to yourself.

Allow others to have their own experiences without attempting to fix things for them. Their soul journey is their own. When you put this into practice, you will feel as strong as a puma and stay healthy.

Fire is the earthly representation of the Sun's energy. Fire ceremonies are very helpful for transmuting energy. Consciously release your emotions, and offer them to the fire. Fire purifies and transforms your thoughts.

Andean Fire Rituals at Willka T'ika

Andean fire rituals stem from the ancient custom of burning special offerings to Pachamama and the Apukuna. Nina, the Andean spirit of fire, supplies the spark for the transformation into Source or the Divinity that lies within all living things. She sustains a driving energy that sets desires, requests and prayers into motion. During the *haywarikuy* ceremonial offering, an exchange of living energy takes place between the ritual specialist, the Apukuna, Pachamama, and Her guests. The spirit world is invited to join the festivities.

The ritual specialist, or *pakko*, prepares the offering. Coca leaves, corn, spices, fragrances, seeds, minerals and symbols of gold and silver are placed on a piece of paper. This "plate" is now filled with Pachamama's favorite products. Prayers, blessings and good intentions are added, and it is sealed. The offering is wrapped inside an *ukuña* (ceremonial woven cloth). This medicine bundle can also be used for healing purposes. The offering is made in anticipation that, in return, Pachamama will bless participants with a productive year, and they will receive all their heart's desires.

The pakko, or *layka* (female healer), moves to an outdoor fire pit where the offering will be burned. Asking permission from the surrounding deities to conduct the ceremony, the Andean pakko dispenses prayers and herbs to purify the site. *Chicha*, a brew made from fermented corn, and floral water may be added. Participants gather around the fire and connect with its active energies. Energy builds from joyful songs, chants, drumming and rattles. When the fire

is ready to receive the offering, the specialist places the bundle into the center of the fire with loving care.

To assure participants that all is well, the pakkos announce whether the spirits of the fire have accepted the offering or not. When the fire relaxes into peaceful, soothing and glowing embers, participants leave the ceremony with feelings of completion and contentment. Ritual specialists remain with the blaze until its fiery spirit burns out.

Songo:
Heart Garden

Sonqo Heart Garden

Sonqo, the heart chakra garden, resonates with heartfelt feelings. In a garden dedicated to *munay*, or love, a loving connection can be experienced with a magnificent flower, a beautiful sunset or a Quechua child expressing pure joy. This garden helps awaken true powers of unconditional love and compassion. When felt in the heart and shared with others, love flourishes then returns.

Heart Chakra: Receives and radiates love; center of emotional response

Meditation symbol: Six-pointed star. "I am open to receive all energy as love."

Andean garden symbol: Coca leaves, an offering of love to Pachamama.

Primary colors: Green and pink, for love and compassion.

Signature Plant of the Heart Garden

Clavel
or Carnation

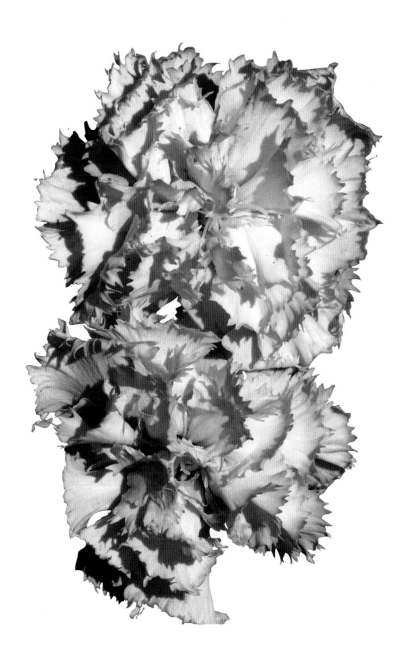

Since carnations are widely known all over the world, I asked a healer to "read the coca leaves," or obtain information for me, from the unified field of intelligence. I wanted to know why carnations have such importance to traditional, Andean healers. The leaves said that long before the Spanish arrived in Peru—*wayra* (the wind) brought clavel to the Andes.

The healer threw the leaves again, then told me this story: *"A long time ago, a shepherdess lost two little lambs. Searching everywhere, she called and called for them until she came to the cave of a wolf, who told her he had eaten them. Frightened and sad, she heard a field filled with clavels singing to her, 'Please don't be sad. The wolf must also eat. Everything is part of Pachamama's process. You cannot judge others.' When she reached home, she asked her father, a wise man, why the carnations had sung to her. He threw his coca leaves and said, 'The vibrations of the clavel open the heart. The flowers were reminding you everyone must eat. People must not be selfish. When you judge, the heart gets sick. When you carry sorrow, you do not allow in love.'"*

Clavel petals drunk in matés are said to draw the love vibration to you and heal the heart. Carnations are widely used for healing today by Andean shamans in offering ceremonies to Pachamama.

Different color vibrations of the clavel relate differently to the heart. White offers eternal peace in love. Magenta enhances wisdom. Intensely fragrant, pink carnations thrive in the Heart Garden. These flowers help transform the mind and heart. They are the perfect signature plant for this garden, a reminder that everything flows from the heart.

Pink and Green Plants of the Heart Garden

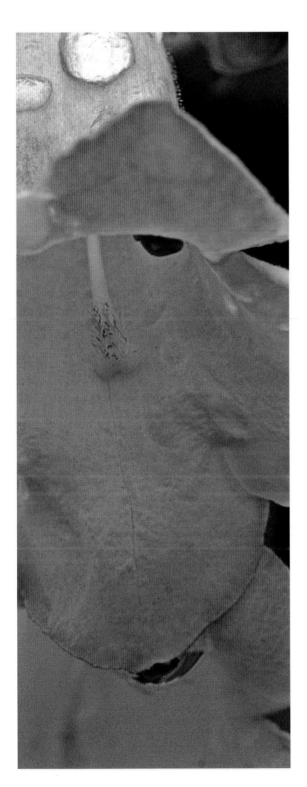

A variety of pink flower peeks through tall green plants surrounding Sonqo's garden. Within the circle of large stones, flowers and a line of energy connect people to Pachamama. Her pink and green vibrations resonate with the rays emanating from their heart centers. In this heartfelt garden of verdant shrubs and blushing flowers, Mother Earth embraces people with Her loving energy while they renew their contact with Nature. Her vibrations of healing and harmony calm the mind and relax the body.

Green, a combination of the warmth of yellow and coolness of blue, calms fatigue, soothes nerves and transmits tranquility. Green is a blend of the yellow power of the solar plexus with the blue self-expression of the throat chakra. True power is love expressed. When people feel envy, or hold any negative vibrations, Nature's green helps calm them down. Pink is a combination of the red of the earth chakra with the white of the crown chakra, which opens to the heavens. When heaven and earth meet in the heart, love

results. Pink flowers in the Heart Garden have a softening quality that purifies the spirit. This helps people work with sensitive issues that affect tender places within their hearts.

To receive energies of love from the earth and sky, plant and animal worlds, people must balance the heart energy center. Gentle and nurturing vibrations of the Heart Garden attract guests, dogs, birds and insects. Those who allow themselves to go deeply within connect on a vibrational level with flowers, grasses, shrubs and all life. They transmit positive vibrations of love into the world, attracting people with similar energy, reflecting the same vibration back to themselves.

Consciously connecting their open hearts with the heart of Nature, people transform their personal desires into loving vibrations. These vibrations positively affect Nature and all of humankind. Always in harmony with humans through their heart chakras, Sonqo is one of the most powerful and supportive energetic gardens at Willka T'ika.

COSMOS

Bright pink cosmos resonate with the heart and help guests express their ideas clearly and lovingly. Encouraging people to maintain a calm disposition, cosmos remind people to be "free spirits."

COCA LEAVES

Coca leaves are of utmost ceremonial importance for healing in the Andes. *Picchar kuka* is the act of chewing coca leaves. Leaves are chewed together with *llipt'a* (a small piece of lime ash), which releases the alkaloids from the leaves and acts as a soft stimulant. Used by the Andean people, the coca leaf has many beneficial effects. It helps the Quechua working at high altitudes to endure long periods without food or sleep. It diminishes the effects of hunger, thirst and fatigue. Healers continuously chew leaves activated by llipt'a. Saliva activates the leaves and extracts Vitamins C and B. Offering prayers, gifted healers are drawn into an alternate state of consciousness, allowing them to perceive the world in a different realm. This brings forth special healing abilities.

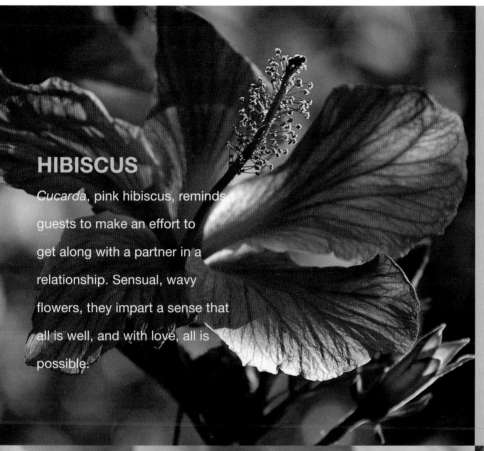

HIBISCUS

Cucarda, pink hibiscus, reminds guests to make an effort to get along with a partner in a relationship. Sensual, wavy flowers, they impart a sense that all is well, and with love, all is possible.

SARA (ANDEAN CORN)

When used in a sacred manner during ceremonies, Andean corn is referred to as "*sara*". Native to the Andes, the green stalks align energetically with the heart of Pachamama. Sara reminds people to stay centered in their bodies. Andean ceremonies include corn kernels, which represent abundance and are said to mirror the soul's desire to live freely in the spaciousness of Nature. Like corn, the physical body grows strong and upright. With a sturdy foundation, it is free to express its vast spiritual nature, opening up to all the world offers. *Chicha*, the nutritious alcoholic beverage made from fermented corn, is used in Andean rituals to honor Pachamama, Apukuna and other deities. Corn remains one of the most important food sources for humans and animals.

GERANIUMS

The magnificent, pink tones found in geraniums leave guests delighted at their beauty. Their vibrations of joy and abundance help the heart manifest its desires.

MUÑA

Muña is a favorite remedy for the prevention
and healing of *sorroche,* (altitude sickness). A
hot tea made with muña's fragrant green leaves
dotted with delicate white flowers and a few
pink or rose carnation petals can soothe the
heart. Muña tea calms the body and brings
peace and tranquility. It is also used to eliminate
headaches or digestive problems. We use
muña oil to keep fleas off the dogs. Muña does
not appear to grow outside of South America.
Scientifically, it is known as *Minthostachys
setosa Briq.*

LEMON BALM

Torongil, melissa or lemon balm, is one of the
most popular Andean healing herbs. Taken
in teas, torongil is thought to alleviate fear,
grief and tension. The Quechua believe the
green leaves make an excellent heart tonic,
regulating the heartbeat, whipping people out
of depression and filling the heart with joy. In
addition to all its attributes, torongil is used to
ensure a good night's sleep so people wake up
feeling rejuvenated. It is easy to grow and does
well in the shade.

Creating the Heart Garden

I frequently sat and meditated on a flat stone lying beneath a small *molle* (Andean pepper tree). A few meters away, a giant, elongated boulder lay covered by dense, thorny, dried-out, rambling roses. After tackling the job of pruning, I rested on the flat stone. Each time I sat upon the stone, I felt peaceful, loving energies swirl in my heart chakra.

My friend Don Benito, a Qero pakko from the snow-covered, sacred mountain, Ausangate, found me there. He stopped to see how I was doing. He handed me gifts of organic potatoes and medicinal plants brought from his far-away village.

Benito nodded approval at my choice of garden seat, telling me it was a good idea to sit beneath a molle tree. He praised the healing properties of its leaves and its ability to remove toxins from the body during healing Andean *baños* (baths). We talked about the weather and crops, two subjects of paramount importance to Andean campesinos. I enjoyed those relaxed meetings with him. They were a wonderful contrast to news from the outside world. Looking at Benito that day, I felt this

garden was connected to the heart. Benito, who invariably had his mouth stuffed with coca leaves, managed a big smile as he nodded his head in agreement. *"Sonqo, sonqo, allin sonqo."* "Good heart." he said, patting his heart chakra, affirming how good it is to stay focused on the positive energies of the heart.

Later, Don Benito and I walked around the

gardens, comparing the valley medicinal plants with plants he brought from his high-altitude, mountain community at 14,000 feet. Intrinsically, Quechua campesinos believe that plants have the ability to heal people on all levels - emotional, mental, physical and spiritual. Willka T'ika's guests often arrive with heavy hearts, seeking peace and healing. Their hearts desire to stay open to love, absorbing

the pure spiritual energies of the gardens and surrounding Sacred Valley sites. At Willka T'ika, our staff provide out-of-sorts guests with medicinal teas or herbal poultices.

Even though they have access to clinics and doctors, most Quechua people consult native healers who offer natural remedies to bring them back into balance. Andean healers often ask patients, "Has something upset you? Do you have relationship problems? How is your heart?" Always, they include flowers and plants to treat the problem.

One of the gardeners told me that huge, natural boulders on the property mysteriously followed an invisible energy line to Inkan ruins, an eight-hour walk up the valley. In the opposite direction, the ley line of energy continued from where I was sitting, past the Lucuma tree to the ancient ceremonial circles at Moray. Unknowingly, by building two guest rooms on the line, we had blocked the energetic path of the boulders.

I wondered how we could repair the damage we had inflicted upon Pachamama's boulders, enigmatically positioned along invisible *seqes*

120 Sonqo: Heart Garden

(lines of energy). Since ancient times, temples and holy sites in Peru have been built on vortices, or spiraling, whirling centers of energy. The ley lines connecting the vortices are said to run along and beneath the earth's surface. Ancient people believed this energy spiritually enhanced holy sites.

In my favorite spot beneath the molle tree, I visualized energy freely flowing beneath areas where building construction had interrupted its path. From my heart, I sent out loving energy to dissolve blockages we might have caused. I believed my intention could assist Nature in her quest to find an alternative route around our construction.

Somehow I knew that a circle of large stones would enhance the energies in the Heart Garden. I asked the workers to move large boulders there. Watching the men sweat and struggle in the process, I was reminded of visits to Inkan temples where guides explain how "thousands" of Inkan men moved 120-ton stones from quarries more than 10 kilometers (6 miles) away. Not only did the Inka cross the Urubamba River with these giant boulders, they "carried" them up mountains and managed to slot them perfectly into place. Watching how challenging it was for the men to maneuver the Heart Garden stones, I remained unconvinced about Inkan, stone-moving theories. I leaned

more toward the theory that ancient Inkans used sound, or other methods, to move stones. In the center of the Heart Garden on the grass, Fabian placed a flat, heart-shaped rock he had found. On the stone, I left giant, spiral-shaped shells with pink, pearly linings; heart-shaped, rose quartz crystals; and rocks I had collected in Africa and Brazil. With its vibrating green and pink hues, crystals, flowers and ancient stones, Sonqo felt peaceful and healing. On a branch of the molle tree, I hung chimes. A basket filled with coca leaves was set out to remind guests to express their love to Pachamama. Filled with love, the soft vibrations of this garden attracted guests into Sonqo. For some, this was the beginning of profound healing.

Summer rains came again. To my delight, cascades of magnificent, pink roses burst forth from the pruned, climbing rose bush and covered the nearby stone wall. Nature's pink and green colors were perfect enhancers to the heart chakra energies. Tall, green grasses growing behind the ring of stones offered privacy to guests enjoying the Heart Garden. Surrounded by fragrant beauty, I continued to send out loving energy to the flowers, insects, birds and trees. I extended the energy to Willka T'ika's employees, guests and those living in the neighborhood. To further enhance Sonqo's vibrations, the gardeners continued to add an assortment of delicate, pink flowers.

Several years ago, a feng shui master, R. D. Chang, visited with a small group. I toured the gardens with him. I was eager to hear what "RD" had to say. He seemed pleased with the energies in Pachamama's Earth and Water gardens. He suggested I open small pathways of energy between the two. When I told him I felt something was lacking in the Sun Garden, RD suggested I expand the chakana by removing some shrubs obstructing energy flows to that area.

Upon entering Sonqo's secluded garden, RD extended his hands, opening to the energy. A great, big smile appeared on his face as he said, "This is perfect. It sits correctly in the heart of your entire property." Now I beamed from ear to ear, because RD did not know that for the first eight years, the garden sat next to our outside wall. Then I bought the land next door. Only then did the garden become the "heart" of the entire property. Pachamama's blueprint for Willka T'ika's gardens was in place long before I knew it or began the physical work of creating each garden.

I recalled how one week after I woke up in California deciding to purchase land in Peru, the land that is now Willka T'ika appeared for sale. When I had to pay for it, a check for the exact amount arrived in the mail. Once I made a firm decision to move to Peru, I could feel support from the Universe. For each step I took, I consulted no one. I avoided conversations with friends or family. I went about my plans offering people a minimum of information. I was determined not to hear others' concerns for me nor did I want their advice.

"...cascades of magnificent, pink roses burst forth from the pruned, climbing rose bush and covered the nearby stone wall. Nature's pink and green colors were perfect enhancers to the heart chakra energies".

I had complete faith that I had chosen the right path for myself, and I was not about to let anyone attempt to cloud the path I had chosen.

I received insights and inspired ideas when I followed my heart. I introduced them into the gardens. I enjoyed working with the quiet, easy-going, young Quechua men, designing each garden in ways that felt right in my heart. As challenges appeared along the way, I accepted them as lessons to learn about myself and the new culture I had chosen to live in. I trusted that there would always be work for me to do in Peru, and filled with determination to follow my path, I moved ahead.

I trusted that my needs would always be met, even when there was little money in my bank account. When I needed money, guests would arrive. As money came in, I continued to use it to expand our work and property. I learned that the government was not supporting school programs, and there were no social services in place to support children in desperate need of assistance. Soon, I became involved in assisting teachers working in isolated, mountain communities. I encouraged guests to contribute money and school supplies to Quechua school children.

Each day, I woke up to greet the Sun coming over the mountains. I looked forward to working with Nature and thoroughly enjoyed the sensation of going with the flow. Just as most children love connecting dot-to-dot to see what the final picture will be, I moved from rock to rock, eager to see how the full garden picture would turn out.

Andean Lore and the Heart Chakra

Ayni is the essence of the heart chakra and true love. "I give to you, and you give to me." The energy of ayni in the heart chakra guides the energies of the first three chakras to create greater good for everyone.

Oral tradition speaks of a time, long, long ago, when the Andean region was filled with pure vibrations of *munay*, unconditional love. It flowed among the interconnected spiritual, mental and physical Andean worlds. Over time, vibrations of fear, envy and greed created wars and violent crime. Pachamama wept for this unloving way of being.

Untouched by the influence of the outside world, Andean pakkos, healers and ritual specialists, became the caretakers of the earth. Living in inhospitable, isolated, mountain communities, they managed to escape the influence of the Spanish invaders and the Catholic Church. They never forgot their connection to Pachamama. Honoring their ancient wisdom, they continue with loving ceremonies and rituals to this day. Nourished by these, Mother Earth sends gifts of love and healing to the hearts of all her people, taking care of them.

The number one question asked of Don Benito when he reads coca leaves, is "When will I meet the man of my dreams?" This is a result of the western belief that love is found outside yourself. Puzzled healers ask me why overseas visitors are always searching for love despite their beauty, charm and apparent wealth. In Andean communities, life seems to be less complicated. At the "right" age, young people fall in love, their families meet to celebrate the union, and the couple starts a family. They work hard on the land and live together for

life. Looking deeper, perhaps energetically the culture and traditions keep them deeply rooted in the first three chakras. As the energy moves to the heart chakra, young campesinos are not romantically striving or searching for a world "out there".

The lesson for modern man is to believe that with love and pure intention, the course of energy on the planet can be changed. With her heart wide open, Pachamama wants us to help her bring balance back to all life. She patiently waits for us to return to love.

The Heart Garden's Chakra

It is the heart chakra that provides an emotional response to all that happens in human lives. How often do people express the words, "I love that person, that story, view, necklace, movie or happy circumstance?" How often do they catch themselves expressing the view that they dislike something, someone, politics, an animal or a room? The energy generated in the heart chakra radiates out and disperses. It affects people and all that surrounds them.

Look at the heart chakra in its relationship to the other chakras. The focus of the root chakra is caring deeply about Pachamama. Because of what lies in the heart center, people make offerings of love and receive nurturance from the earth. When the heart chakra is open, ayni takes care of the earth, people and everything around them.

People resonate with the flow of sacral chakra energies which stimulate their creativity in its many forms. Because of what lies in the heart center, passion and ideas burst forth. When the heart is open, people do not withhold their ideas. They "brainstorm" with others to exchange them. An open heart directs creative energy in a positive manner.

As life force becomes active in the solar plexus chakra, people are "fired-up," physically energized. An open heart chakra turns this energy into enthusiastic and positive action. Practicing ayni, people share their ideas with others, and insights return to them. This leads to the creation of further enriched ideas.

Sonqo, the heart chakra, takes on the energies of all the previous chakras and puts them to work in relationships with people, animals and all of nature. It is the first of the chakras to turn fundamental energies into life actions and attitudes. To a large extent, this chakra determines what is done in the remaining chakras. It guides people in the way they accomplish things.

When a person's heart chakra fills with love, it radiates out into the surrounding universe, which reflects and returns that love to the person who sent it. By contrast, if a person's heart chakra is filled with concern, fear, blame and dislike, then that is what life around the person reflects and what returns to the person.

The heart chakra serves as a portal leading into higher vibrational frequencies where matter changes into energy, and everything begins to resonate at a higher level. As young people mature into their late twenties, their hearts expand to engage people in warm, spontaneous and caring relationships. The more awakened the heart, the greater the capacity for experiencing undemanding spiritual love.

On a physical level, the heart chakra corresponds to the heart and lungs. Air is the breath of life, clear and undulating. It comes in and goes out. It gives and receives. Air brings in oxygen for physical energy and returns carbon dioxide to feed the plant cycle of life. Breath is a powerful tool for change. In the Andes, the physical equivalent of yogic prana is *kausay* (the energy that gives life). How we use that energy passing through us affects everything. The heart must be open for there to be communication between inner wisdom, rooted in past experience, and the higher wisdom of divine Source. Nature encourages us to open our hearts wide to perceive beauty and spiritual love in all fellow human beings, providing emotional wellbeing.

Power of the Heart Garden

The traditional practice of ayni is about love. This custom is deeply woven into the fabric of the earth-based, spiritual practices of the Quechua. It is centered on unconditional love for Pachamama. It is based on honoring Mother Earth. For thousands of years, it has kept communities healthy and in harmony with Nature. When the practice of ayni is abandoned, the flow of cosmic energy centered around the heart chakra becomes blocked. Today, the Quechua are faced with the challenge of finding a way to blend new ways of living with their timeless, heart-centered practice of ayni.

Visitors from other lands continue to come to the Andes to experience the pure energy and loving vibrations that are still held in place. They come to experience a deep connection to Pachamama, whose loving energies nourish the heart and soul. When they participate in offerings to Pachamama, She flourishes. In the true spirit of ayni, those who participate also flourish. With heart chakras wide open, they leave the Andes feeling spiritually renewed.

Since outer experience reflects inner thoughts, if something in the outer world is not the way we want it to be, it can be changed.

Focus on the heart, thoughts, feelings and spending time in Nature. This has the power to change our experience. True intimacy comes when we open our hearts widely enough to feel the support of Divine energies. They provide us with all we need in the most appropriate way.

One woman shared her experience in the Heart Garden: *"Personal growth work taught me I could choose what would dominate me. I was shocked to realize my need to avoid being controlled was controlling me! This pattern had been in place for more than fifty years – a result of being beaten by my father while growing up. Meditating quietly in the Heart Garden, I 'heard' the garden ask me, 'Is your heart big enough to love your father?' 'Yes,' I answered, choosing to be dominated by love. A profound healing occurred, and I felt the forgiveness work with my father was complete."*

New Patterns of Thinking and Feeling

Sonqo reminds everyone to experience and release emotions such as grief, fear, judgment and worry. Emotions are vibrational energies. Emotional blockage in the heart is caused by not grieving the loss of someone or something dear. Failing to acknowledge aspects of life that cause pain also blocks the heart chakra. Blockages of unaddressed emotions may turn into physical ailments.

Becoming aware of unwanted heart chakra patterns and releasing them clears the space for love and happiness. Love is acceptance of people and conditions exactly the way they are and not how you wish they would be. Emotions are part of being human. Allowing emotions to be, rather than resisting them, helps them dissipate. Resistance gives negative energy to emotions, keeping them in place. Acknowledging and appreciating emotions frees them to go.

OLD PATTERNS	NEW THOUGHT PATTERNS
Anger	I take complete responsibility for my experience. I am a powerful creator.
Blame, resentment	I forgive myself. I forgive others. I am deeply and profoundly forgiven.
Fear	I know the Universe loves and supports me. I trust in Spirit.
Worry	I stay present. I am safe.
Stress	I surrender to the flow of divine energy knowing all is welll

Meditation on the Six-pointed Star

"I am open to receive all energies as infinite love."

Upon entering Sonqo's garden, offer a gift, a prayer or three coca leaves in loving acknowledgement of Pachamama and the spirits of this garden. Take a moment to express gratitude for Her beauty which surrounds and supports you. Let the loving energies fill you.

Close your eyes and visualize the six-pointed star placed above your heart chakra. Breathe the pure air coming from Hanakpacha, the upper spiritual world. Draw the breath into your heart. Breathe out, feeling the breath move down into the earth. Breathe into your heart, feeling the nurturing energies of Ukhupacha, the inner world. Breathe out into the upper world.

With the star symbol in your mind, breathe into your heart chakra. Release the energies from your heart to everything around you. Repeat the process a few times.

In this moment, ask yourself, "What am I feeling?" Acknowledge the feeling in your heart. If there is sadness, continue the process a little longer, breathing the sadness out from your heart.

Continue to relax deeply. Breathe until you feel pure loving vibrations. Experience a sense of interconnection with the entire universe.

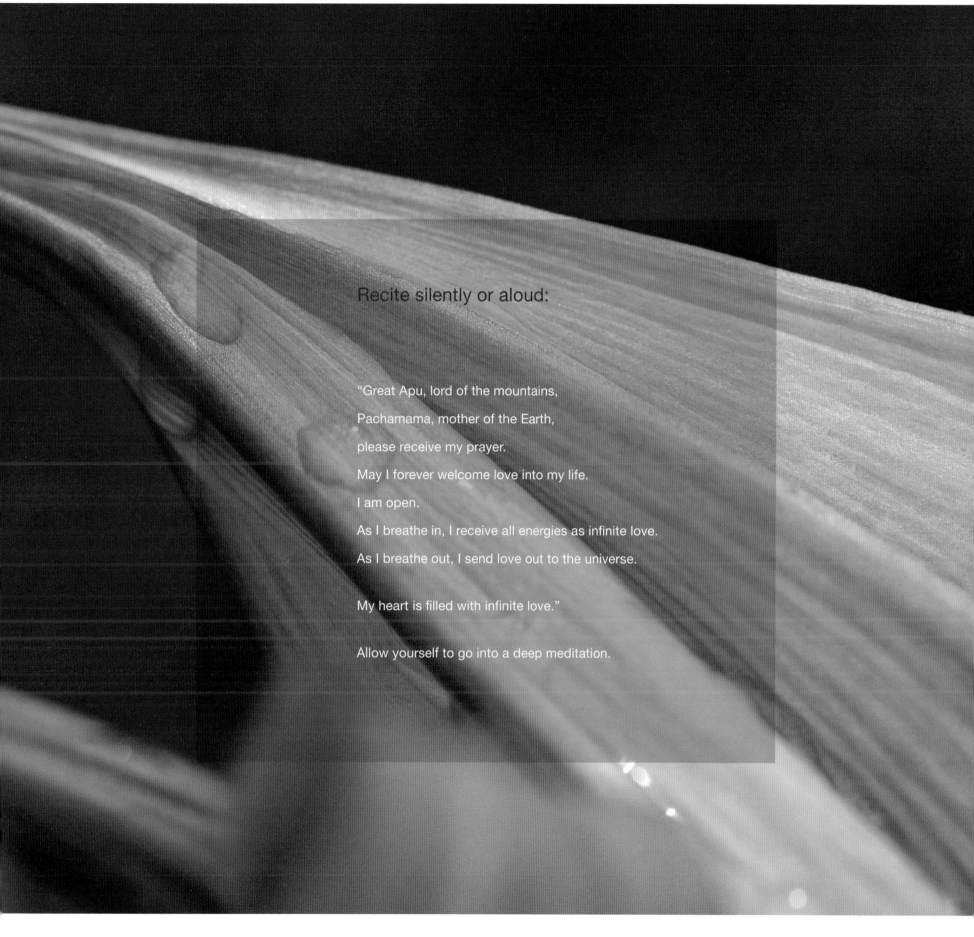

Recite silently or aloud:

"Great Apu, lord of the mountains,

Pachamama, mother of the Earth,

please receive my prayer.

May I forever welcome love into my life.

I am open.

As I breathe in, I receive all energies as infinite love.

As I breathe out, I send love out to the universe.

My heart is filled with infinite love."

Allow yourself to go into a deep meditation.

Flower or Plant Meditation

Sit next to a flower or plant of your choice. Acknowledge its presence, and send it love. Open your heart to receive its vibrations. Look deeply at it. Note its colors, patterns, shapes, fragrance and texture. Ask it to connect with your heart. Close your eyes. Imagine yourself getting smaller, small enough to go within the flower, close to its heart. Wait for it to speak. Listen deeply. It may wish to share messages with you. If you have a question, ask it, and wait for an answer. It may come from a different realm. Be open to receive this wisdom. When you are ready, leave the flower, and return to the present. Open your eyes. Offer gratitude and deep thanks.

You may wish to draw or paint the flower or write in your journal. Hold the image you have of the flower, and see it as an expression of light and energy. When you feel complete, offer thanks to the flower or plant.

Color Meditation in Sonqo's Garden

Hold a piece of rose quartz in your hand. Feel the color flow naturally into your heart center. Choose a soft pink rose or any flower that speaks to your heart. Meditate, and draw nature's green color into your heart. Allow the natural healing energies of balance and harmony to nourish you. Observe how your heart feels. As you bring the energy of love into your heart center, visualize the pink color of love caressing your heart.

Invite garden spirits to draw close to you. Feel their soft, pink light and healing energy surround you and fill your body. Relax and be at peace. Affirm: "I feel the vibrations of the pink flower and rose quartz crystal filling my heart with gentle, loving, healing energies." Express gratitude for all you have in your life. Be open and receptive to any messages from Nature.

Ceremony in the Heart Garden

Sit in the Heart Garden and express gratitude for all you have. Acknowledge the beauty around you. Let joyful vibrations fill your heart.

Feel your heart filling with compassion. Speak from your heart. Resonate with others at the heart level. Feel a deep connection with your Divine Source. Start with one minute. Expand to one hour, then to one day. Begin with yourself.

Create your own heart chakra garden. From neglected land filled with thorns and rocks, I created a beautiful garden. In time it transformed into a garden of love. The same energies are available to you. Use them. Fill your own garden with roses and heart-shaped, pink quartz crystals or other jewels from the earth. Allow these natural elements to soothe you and bring joy to your heart. Flowers need space to bloom and grow, and so do you.

Yogic Relaxing Exercise to De-stress

The tongue is an amazing on-off switch. Yogis teach that the tongue is the first muscle to tense up with worry, throwing off breathing and affecting the heart center. Simply sit, close your eyes, drop your jaw and let your tongue hang out. Inhale through your nose, and exhale through your mouth. Repeat this a few times, exhaling with the sound "aahh". As your shoulders drop and your back relaxes, your rib cage will expand, your pulse will slow and your blood pressure may drop. Your heart opens. Observe how you instantly feel centered and calmer. Seize this moment to focus your thoughts on what you want, and hold that vibration. The Heart Garden is a perfect place to release worry and stress.

Takiwasi:

Sound Garden

Takiwasi: Sound Garden

Vibrational sound patterns brought the universe into being. The throat chakra resonates with the sounds of the universe. Takiwasi is a garden house dedicated to sounds, chanting and music. The sounds of Nature reverberate within the garden. Blue and turquoise colors stimulate the throat chakra. The Sound Garden calls people to speak with confidence to the world. Clusters of turquoise and aquamarine flowers outline Takiwasi's round ceremonial hut. Sound Garden flowers in shades of azure blue, indigo and sapphire resonate with throat chakra vibrations. When people say, "It came out of the blue," they are referring to information from the Universe. A person with an open throat chakra fully resonates and communicates with dynamic energy moving within and around them at all times. Communication with garden spirits, spirit teachers, angels or ancestors takes place in the spiritual realm.

Sounds, and vibrations from blue and turquoise flowers infuse the Sound Garden with powerful, healing energy. They have a soothing effect on the body. Guided imagery, with sounds and colors, has helped stroke patients improve their speech coordination. Medical personnel wear healing blue in operating rooms. Patients listening to selected music report diminished pain during surgery. Nature offers many healing benefits through sound and color vibrations. Sounds emanating from crystal and Tibetan bowls in Takiwasi's meditation room flow to meet wind chimes and harmonize with Nature's breezes. Fine notes vibrate, resonate, reverberate and attract answering sounds and harmonies. The expression "to strike a true note" suggests that people draw synchronicities toward themselves while disharmonies are reduced. Takiwasi's indoor walls carry the inscription *OM* from different cultures. OM symbolizes the beginning and completion of creation, the world beyond form. Chanting OM directs sound energy from the head downwards into the belly. Harmonious sound waves expand the energy field, bringing people into balance.

Communication among humans, plants, animals and universal energies exists on different levels. When people look deeply at Nature, and listen to Her, they open to meaningful messages or insights. Animals speak to humans in dreams. Dogs know when people need comforting.

A sound garden becomes a singing garden. Guests may pause to ask if they have stopped singing their personal song, the sound of their creative soul. Filled with the vibrations of sky-blue flowers, chanting, singing, drumming and Pachamama's creations, they can link with the sounds and harmonies of the universe. Expressing delight and gratitude through singing and chanting keeps the throat center open and balanced. The repetitive chanting of sound sends messages of wellbeing through the psychic and physical nervous systems, reinforcing the healing of wounds retained in the cellular memory.

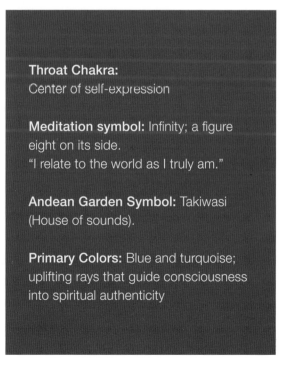

Throat Chakra:
Center of self-expression

Meditation symbol: Infinity; a figure eight on its side.
"I relate to the world as I truly am."

Andean Garden Symbol: Takiwasi (House of sounds).

Primary Colors: Blue and turquoise; uplifting rays that guide consciousness into spiritual authenticity

Signature Plant of the Sound Garden

Tarwi

Strong-spirited Andean *tarwi*, its sky-blue flowers tinged with light turquoise and yellow, self-seeds in the Andean mountains. It is the signature plant of the Sound Garden because it is said to help the throat chakra open to spirituality, allowing wisdom to flow. The spoken word is powerful. It can create or destroy. When people use their words for positive communication, consciousness transforms. Often referred to as an Incan legume, the raw tarwi bean is recommended by naturopaths for many uses. High in protein, tarwi is popular as a nutritious and delicious food.

AFRICAN LILY,
OR LILY OF THE NILE

Blue and turquoise *agapanthus africanus*, or lily of the Nile, remind people to speak wisely, clearly and honestly. In my Johannesburg and California gardens, agapanthus flowers bloomed for a short time each year. In the Andes, they continue to flower month after month, seeming to shout reminders to people to share right speech with integrity.

BORAGE

In Willka T'ika's gardens, prolific borage shrubs explode with blossoms year round. Their uplifting blue hues fill guests with courage and calm the mind. When people feel discouraged or experience a heavy heart, the delicate blue flowers lighten the energy and encourage them to speak with optimism. Borage plants are said to stimulate the adrenal glands to produce adrenaline, the "fight or flight" hormone. This readies the body for action in stressful situations and may stimulate it to produce its own natural cortisone to build the immune system. High in vitamin C, borage flowers are used in tea or syrup for calming fear, anxiety, coughs and colds. Boiled leaves and flowers are used in lotions to treat skin conditions, rashes and insect bites. The chefs patiently harvest tiny borage flowers to decorate salads and cakes, transforming them into works of art.

FORGET-ME-NOT

"Forget-me-not," whisper tiny blue flowers, reminding souls of their spiritual and karmic connections with others. The vibrations of these flowers are said to aid with the release of feelings of loneliness, guiding souls to a higher level of heart exchange.

LARKSPURS AND DELPHINIUM

Larkspurs and delphinium proudly display their tall, flower-filled stalks in rich hues of blue. Lavish flower vibrations enthusiastically and charismatically encourage people to inspire with their words, leading and motivating others to do the same.

PLUMBAGO

Walking through Urubamba's market one day, I was delighted to find a small *cerrato,* or plumbago plant, growing in a plastic bag. Nearly thirty years ago, when I began my spiritual quest, I did not trust my intuition and found it difficult to make decisions for myself. Whenever I felt indecisive or in doubt during the next few years, I took the flower essence of cerrato. I never looked back. I had no further problems deciding what I wanted to do. I made sure the hardy, fast-spreading shrub—with masses of blue, clustered flowers—had a place of honor in all my subsequent gardens. Some gardeners regard the shrub as a weed, but to me, whenever I walk past pretty, blue cerrato flowers, I pause and look deeply at them. They remind me to trust my inner being.

BLUE SALVIA

Blue *salvia,* from the sage plant, guides people to choose their direction wisely. Their flower vibrations inspire people to review their life's progress from a higher perspective. This generous plant enhances the capacity to experience deep inner peace and wisdom.

SWEET PEAS

Gorgeous, fragrant, blue sweet peas thrive during colder months at Willka T'ika's 9,000-foot altitude. All-time favorites that bring instant joy, sweet peas send messages of wellness, abundance and determination to those who walk in their midst.

Creating the Sound Garden

The Sacred Valley is blessed with spectacular beauty and agreeable climate year round. Fertile land and spiritual energy drew pre-Inkan people to the valley. Quechua farmers and I were drawn to the land for many of the same reasons. Grateful to own a flat piece of land for gardening in the heart of the Sacred Valley, I welcomed each Andean day.

After three years of experimenting with native herbs and flowers, I broke with Andean tradition. I began to cultivate exotic varieties of medicinal plants, edible flowers and gourmet salads, instead of corn, potatoes, lettuce and cabbage. Guest cottages, yoga studios and meditation rooms were upgraded and expanded. Yoga and special interest groups arrived to enjoy Willka T'ika as part of their journey to Machu Picchu.

One winter day, while taking a break from the hot, midday sun, I sat under the thatched roof of an open hut. It did not have a welcoming energy even though herbs and flowers surrounded it. Fabian, a Quechua staff member, joined me. I asked him for ideas to improve the area. After a minute or two, he looked at me and said, "Close it in." "What a great idea!" I thought. The picture of an indoor ceremonial area where healers could conduct ceremonies flashed through my mind. With a view of the mountains and a cozy fireplace for winter nights, this appeared to be the perfect place.

In a very short time, the round, open hut transformed into a joyful place. I gathered an assortment of Andean and Amazonian drums, rattles, reeds and flutes. The enclosed hut morphed into a *takiwasi*, house of sounds. Guests were encouraged to borrow instruments for outdoor fire ceremonies. Sounds of music added joyful energies to the dancing fire spirits during the *haywarikuy* offering ceremony to Pachamama.

Takiwasi became a favorite area for shamanic and Buddhist meditation groups. Fireplace shelves filled with gongs, bowls, old stones and crystals. They amplified the energy. With chanting, singing and sound vibrations pouring into the surrounding gardens, we turned our focus to Nature. We prepared garden beds along paths to the new, round room. Instinctively, I planted blue agapanthus tubers from my native South Africa. We surrounded them with cuttings, seeds and herbs that soon produced flowers ranging from sky blue to deep turquoise. By spring, we proudly acknowledged the perfection of Takiwasi's singing garden. We thanked Pachamama for providing this garden to resonate with the throat chakra of each person who came to intermingle with Her nature spirits.

Andean Lore and the Sound Garden

More than 5,000 years ago, haunting sounds of the *wankar, tinta, alzon, antara, zampona and kena* (ancient musical instruments) were played in holy ceremonies and festivals throughout the Andes. Encompassing an immense range of complicated chromatic scales and half steps, the music reflected the psyche of *Tawantinsuyo*, the Andean world extending from Argentina to Colombia. Phenomenal tones emanated from these intricate wooden instruments. They were believed to resonate with certain giant stones of ancient temples. It was also believed their sounds moved stones. Alive with images, sounds echo movements of Nature, filling the soul with Her vibrations.

Magnificent stone chambers built alongside the holy temples at Machu Picchu suggest that before entering, priests and priestesses used the trapezoidal, stone niches to tune, harmonize and balance their chakras. They leaned forward into the niches and chanted. Their voices resonated in a deep, rich, perfect pitch that sent ripples of flowing energy down their spines and through the chakras. The giant, spiral-shelled *patuta* (conch), harvested from the Pacific Ocean and carried to holy temples throughout the land, summoned the people to honor and worship Nature with its penetrating sound.

Music remains an integral part of the Andean world. Vibrant **waynas** (songs that have been passed down for centuries) can be heard at all fiestas and ceremonies. The rhythm and beat of an Andean song expresses mythology, mountains and moonlight. It is a remarkable, unforgettable, melodic experience difficult for those who live in cities far away from Nature to appreciate. Andean music is created by villages that see the whole world as a living being.

During Andean ceremonies, pakkos effortlessly use mantras (sacred sounds) to call on the spirit of the Apukuna for protection and purification of the mind and emotions. Used inwardly or spoken aloud, sound vibrations carry pakkos deeper into a relaxed, altered state of consciousness where they connect with the spirit world for healing purposes.

While writing my original book on Andean spiritual wisdom, *Pachamama's Children*, now called *Journey to Machu Picchu,* I interviewed a 95-year-old Quechua man, Faustino Navarro, who traced his lineage back to the Inka. Fully lucid, he spent hours telling me stories and talking about the language he loved so much. In that book, I wrote, "Rich in expression and imagery, *kkechuwa* (Quechua) is the beautiful living language of the Andes. Power resides in the sound of every word. In Peru, the vibration of every sacred peak, landmark, town, river, animal and plant is contained in the language. The sound became the word. For example, words related sounds of weather. *K'kayka* is the clap of thunder produced by lightning. *Para-para* is the sound of falling raindrops. Traditional Quechua people used sounds to summon the power of those objects." Fifteen years later, I was delighted that Nature guided me to dedicate a garden to sound vibrations. Each time I sat in the Sound Garden, a wave of peace and joy washed over me as I resonated with the creation of the Universe.

Review of the Throat Chakra

The chakra gardens at Willka T'ika lead visitors from nurturing earth to flowing water. The Sun garden sparks their active fire, and the beat of their hearts sends loving energies into all that surrounds them. When the throat chakra is open, it connects the heart to the head, moving people into a higher frequency where they communicate inspiring ideas to the world. Filled with the purified energies of the other chakras, people can make themselves heard by speaking with complete honesty and an open heart. Words vibrate with beauty and compassion.

The gift of this energy center is truth. Telling the truth about everything empowers people. Sharing their own truths, while respectfully hearing the truths of others, reflects spiritual maturity. They are able to express their passion and creativity in a positive way. When they hear truth, they are open and willing to change their minds.

By focusing on constructive goals, people create positive circumstances for themselves and those around them. Filled with loving vibrations, their thoughts and words enter the universal field of energy where they magnetically attract similar vibrations back to themselves for positive results.

Physicians and holistic practitioners use the power of sound to relax and heal patients. Sound conducts through water, so it is easily carried through the physical body—which contains more than 70% water. Sound waves used in medical procedures are known to reduce tension. Like the breath, sound heals you at the cellular level. When you practice listening to your body's signals, you become open to receive higher wisdom.

Thoughts are vibrations that carry healing intent, enabling energy healing and prayers from a distance to create positive results. Sound, color, breath work, yoga and meditation all are helpful in releasing blocked energy. These simple techniques, added to Nature's pure vibrations in the chakra gardens, create immense shifts in your body and mind, realigning them with your spirit in perfect balance or wholeness.

Power of the Sound Garden

Takiwasi, the Sound Garden, resonates with throat chakra energy. It gives people an opportunity to focus on aspects of their self-expression. Self-expression encompasses responsibility, truth and integrity. To be healthy, people must learn to take full responsibility for their actions in all they say and do. Only when people speak truthfully, with integrity, will they heal certain aspects of their lives. They know they are speaking the truth when they feel the emotion inside, and the feeling is good. When they openly express their feelings with great enthusiasm, their creative spirit comes forth, showing who they really are.

Carolyn describes what came forth for her: *"Carol began by giving a tour of the Chakra Gardens during our first morning. I listened carefully and was intrigued. In the Sound Garden, as she was talking, I found that tears were streaming down my cheeks. The garden's energy knew I needed help with a long-standing thyroid condition. I visited that garden every morning. During the first few visits, I was teary and overwhelmed. I sat quietly each day and was simply filled with peace."* She recently wrote, *"I'm quite well and must say that between the garden experiences and Benito (Andean shaman), I have had no thyroid problem since the night he worked with me."*

I allowed myself to receive the gift of this garden by being true to myself. I decided to make changes that centered on my throat chakra. I taught myself to stay focused on what I wanted and to let go of what I did not want in my life. During construction, when money was lost because of mistakes, I took responsibility for removing my attention from the mistakes and for concentrating on what we needed to do to repair them. I made a conscious effort not to blame. I made a conscious effort to distance myself from anyone whose energy and integrity felt incompatible with mine. The moment I chose and followed this path, the Universe stepped in to draw compatible people to me. Once I understood that it was up to me to create the life I wanted, everything fell into place. In the Sound Garden, joyful sounds reverberating from takiwasi are constant reminders that only clear and truthful vibrations can bring happiness.

Negative television news reports from around the world bring negative vibrations into homes.

When people see violence or hear adverse words, it can affect their physical bodies. Words have great power.

Words can be hurtful or cause resentment. Being honest is not an excuse for people to be unkind to others. It is essential for people to find ways to communicate without demeaning themselves or others.

Meditation in the Sound Garden

Yogis recommend that before you say or do anything, first take a breath. Respond to any question or "charged" statement with, "Just a moment, please." There is always time to take a breath or two. It gives you a precious moment to think about how you choose to respond. A breath offers you a chance to choose your words carefully.

People forget to take time to use their breathing abilities to calm themselves down. Breathing helps people meditate. Breathing is at the core of yoga practice. Take a breath as you say a loving word. Draw love into your heart. In the Sound Garden, breathe in the delicious fragrances of flowers.

Yogis always have understood that breathing helps a body heal at the cellular level. Your nose has an intricate and ingenious air-filtering system. With every cleansing breath consciously taken through the nose, the throat chakra begins to open up and heal. When you breathe through your mouth, you create a panic response which produces adrenaline to notify your body you are in crisis. When you focus on breathing through your nose, your body relaxes and adrenaline is lowered, leaving you less stressed.

To release negative energy consciously, simply pause, breathe and focus on something precious, a person or experience that brings love and joy. Generate positive feelings for yourself and the universe by focusing on what you really want.

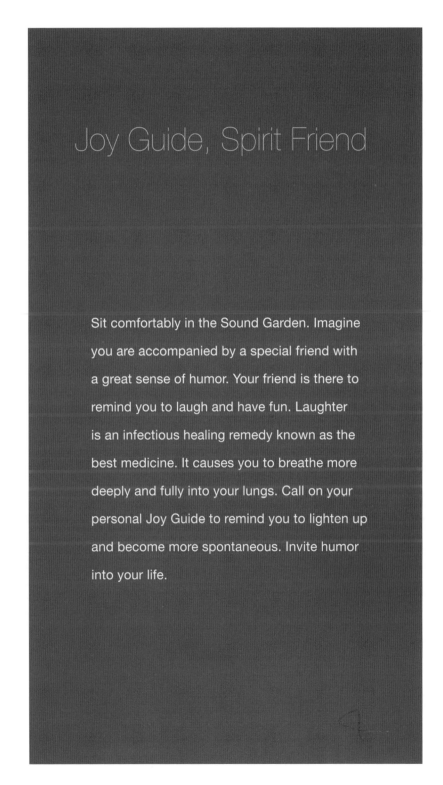

Joy Guide, Spirit Friend

Sit comfortably in the Sound Garden. Imagine you are accompanied by a special friend with a great sense of humor. Your friend is there to remind you to laugh and have fun. Laughter is an infectious healing remedy known as the best medicine. It causes you to breathe more deeply and fully into your lungs. Call on your personal Joy Guide to remind you to lighten up and become more spontaneous. Invite humor into your life.

Meditation on the Infinity Symbol

"I relate to the world with truth and integrity."

Mentally place the infinity symbol above the throat.

This represents limitless, free-flowing spiritual energy. When the throat chakra, the energy center of truth, is open and flowing, feel your connection to Divine Source Energy. Close your eyes.

Affirm:

I focus on honesty and integrity in all that I say and do.

I relate with confidence to the world as I truly am.

I speak truthfully, from my heart.

What I have to say is worthy of being listened to.

I am joyful in my self-expression and creative pursuits.

I see and feel myself connected to Source Energy.

I sound my true note to attract compatible friends and companions toward me.

I see and feel how it is to be surrounded by wonderful friends and special companions.

Sound Garden Ceremony

Beneath the blue sky in the Sound Garden, surrounded by blue and turquoise flowers, breathe in shades of blue. Feel the serenity it brings. Exhale, visualizing the color passing through your throat, tongue and ears. Blue shades fortify each area of the throat chakra. Express yourself truthfully with compassion for yourself and others. Chant OM and the vowel sounds.

Sing or harmonize in tune to your favorite music. Hum, whistle or laugh. Note how your body feels.

Spiral Garden

166 Spiral Garden

Spiral Garden

Walking the spiral garden is an experience in moving deeper into expanding consciousness. Following their heartfelt desires, people journey into higher planes of awareness. Dancing in spiral formation, indigo, lilac, and purple flowers resonate with the third-eye chakra, an opening to intuition and spiritual reflection.

The spiral garden merges the productive energy of Nature with Spirit. Energy moves in spirals to shape the galaxies, countless suns and solar systems. Within the cells of every living thing, spiraling DNA strings energize the micro-universe. The spiral is both the form and symbol of the energy of life. It resembles life's journey.

Each personal, inner journey in the Spiral Garden encourages you to connect to a realm of unlimited knowledge and profound wisdom. This chakra garden assists you in opening to intuition and divine knowledge. Vibrations of richly-colored flowers in lilac hues and of indigenous herbal plants lead you gently on paths that follow the spiral movement of the southern hemisphere. A central vortex, filled with crystals charged with energies from the beginning of time, synchronizes you with the rhythm of the earth.

Third-eye Chakra: Ajna (Center of Light); seat of clairvoyance and intuition.

Meditation symbol: Triangle pointing upward. "Love, Power, Wisdom."

Andean Garden Symbol: *Espiral* (spiral), *kuntur* (condor).

Primary colors: Indigo, lilac, purple.

Indigo Plants of the Spiral Garden

Swirling shades of indigo, lilac, lavender, mauve and purple flowers reveal the giant Spiral Garden. These colors are said to be the highest energy of visible light. They form the boundary between the seen and the unseen. Their vibrations may bring clear insights and greater awareness to people. Blends of lilac, mauve and indigo are regarded as colors of universal healing. Educator Rudolf Steiner said magenta—a mixture of red, green and violet—is the color of ultimate creativity. The red in magenta carries the energy of a strong life force; the green, peace, balance and neutrality; and the violet, spiritual softness. The colors of the Spiral Garden are worn and used by many mediums and healers. They are said to raise levels of consciousness. These color vibrations balance physical and emotional energies in the body. Color therapists warm the cool vibrations of these colors by introducing shades of yellow and orange. Nature does this automatically in the spiral garden. Her magnificent palette offers petals dabs of yellow, orange and white.

Mother Earth's creative processes never move in straight lines. They spiral in natural patterns of movement. The spiral can be seen in the form of the ceremonial Andean *patuta*, or conch, shell, on insects and in mineral stones. People marvel at spirals of growth in many of Willka T'ika's garden plants.

Signature Plant of the Spiral Garden

Kantu

Willka T'ika, or Sacred Flower

Kantu is the name of Willka T'ika's sacred flower. It is the signature plant of the Spiral Garden. Kantu flowers appear on ancient ceramics and textiles. With its variety of magenta-tinged, trumpet-like flowers, kantu's exquisite beauty adorned Inkan women and their palaces.

The spirit of this flower flies with the *picaflores* (hummingbirds) that carry its essence throughout the gardens. Their joyful energies uplift the human heart. Kantu flowers are important elements in Andean ceremonial offerings. Traditional Quechua women still use these flowers to decorate their hats. Kantu flowers encourage people to speak from their hearts and display their inner beauty.

CHIVES

Cebollas chinitos, spindly chives with purple flowers, find a welcome home within the spiral. Spring into the spiral for this herb. Besides adding a zing to salads, chives encourage those partial to onion-flavored foods to keep eating. Chives are believed by valley residents to lower blood pressure and cholesterol, and to act as a mild natural antibiotic.

BOUGAINVILLEA

Generous shades of purple *bougainvillea* carry a vibration of enthusiastic, spiritual wellbeing,

inspiring people to take a spiritual journey to mystical destinations.

GRANADILLA

The growth movement of the *granadilla*, a luscious South American passion fruit, mirrors the spiral pattern of this garden. It has extraordinarily beautiful indigo flowers that spiral their way into the highest of trees. Granadilla has many healing benefits. Its delicious, vitamin-filled fruit is said to work with the intestinal flora in the body.

Granadilla loves to tap into spring water that is not easy to find in the Andes. At Willka T'ika, it has tapped into the fresh springs beneath the land, and this may explain why fruits that normally grow only on tropical farms at low elevations are thriving at Willka T'ika.

IMPATIENS

Trabajadores, multi-colored, water-loving flowers known in English as impatiens, are hard workers, similar to the Quechua people who know about patience and work. Their perky flowers, with striking violet and lilac petals, seem to remind people to accept the flow of life patiently.

IRIS

Most gardeners welcome the beauty of the flowering iris, for it inspires the soul to connect deeply with higher realms. As people meditate next to this magnificent flower in the center of the spiral, new vision and perspectives arise. Creative juices begin to flow. Irises encourage humans to be sparkling, alive, and to remain in harmony with the soul of Pachamama.

MORNING GLORIES

Purple morning glory flowers open to greet the dawn. Their slim stalks spiral into the nooks and crannies of surrounding stone walls until they disappear. These flowers are said to inspire and renew people spiritually, especially if the person is prone to toxic or addictive stimulants. Before closing at each sunset, the morning glories bring in a vital force to awaken and restore faith in spirituality.

PANSIES

Pensamientos, meaning "thoughts", are pansies. These flowers are said to help people share who they are without fear of criticism and failure. Velvety, deep purple and vibrantly-colored flowers appear to be shy and sensitive. They remind people to quiet the mind so they can feel a loving, spiritual connection with Nature. Self-seeders, they continue to bloom in the spiral garden almost all year round.

SWEET PEAS

Fragrant masses of purple sweet peas, filled with spiral tendrils, remind people of the importance of commitment to their community or *ayllu.* Those who are not part of a family or community may find themselves searching for a sense of connectedness. They can reconnect to Nature through this magnificent flower's vibrations, which remind them of the spiral journey of their soul.

TINTIN-TUMBA

Commonly known by its Spanish name, *tumba* climbs into the Andean cherry trees that surround the Spiral Garden. It generously produces its vitamin-filled fruit in summer. *Tintin* has many positive qualities. Its vibrational force is always spiraling upward toward the light. The Quechua use the fruit to help with digestive problems. It is also used ceremonially for depression.

Build a small fire filled with aromatic plants. It's important the smoke not bother tintin's delicate flowers or leaves. During a full moon, meditate near tintin. Look at the spiraling, upward growth pattern of the plant. Place your hands over your heart, and know the depression will spiral up in the smoke.

Creating the Spiral Garden at Willka T'ika

Walking through the gardens one morning, on my way to meditate beneath the lucuma tree, I wondered what to plant in a large area. From nowhere, a swoosh of energy seemed to enter my forehead as I heard a message. "Build a spiral." I sat down on a nearby rock and stared at the empty land. I had no idea how to begin or what size spiral to build. After sitting and staring at nothing for a while, I went to retrieve a pendulum from my house. Ready to consult Nature with my questions, I walked to what I thought was the center of the land. I asked Nature if that was correct. The pendulum swung into "yes." I looked toward the east where the sun rose over the mountains. I asked for confirmation that the spiral should begin on the east side of the land. That too was affirmed.

Now the important question was how wide to make each path in the spiral. Focused on getting answers, I asked whether the paths within the spiral should be two feet wide. The pendulum said "no." I continued to ask if it should be three, four or five feet wide. Each time I received a "no." Thinking the pendulum would continue to stay with "no," I half-heartedly asked about a six-foot width.

Surprised, I watched as the pendulum swung into a resounding "yes." That seemed rather large to me, but I accepted the guidance.

I was delighted to see the completed spiral, eighty-five feet in diameter with six-foot-wide paths, fit beautifully into the land. There was even sufficient space to walk outside the spiral. This was a great moment for me. I could feel Pachamama's presence guiding me in my unusual garden endeavors. Creative ideas flowed. The spiral measurements would allow four feet of space to grow medicinal herbs and flowers within each path. On each side of the flowers, guests would have the opportunity to walk the spiral path. I thanked Pachamama.

As winter months turned to spring, small plants in the spiral sprouted quickly. Cuttings turned into mini-plants. It became clear that Spiral Garden energy helped these plants grow faster and healthier than other cuttings we had planted. One day, I laughed to myself when I heard Lucio, one of the Quechua workers, turn to Fabian and say, "Take it to the hospital," about moving a sickly-looking plant to the Spiral Garden. They were beginning to

understand the special, spiral energy at work.

I continued to plant flowers. The young men, regarding flowers as impractical, filled available space with vegetables. The Quechua still follow this practice today. Wherever there is empty space, they plant a vegetable or two. When I grow geraniums in a *raki* (ceramic pot), someone slips a tomato, celery or parsley seed into the same raki. There always is space for beautiful flowers to grow close to edible plants. For me, this makes the gardens even more interesting. Whenever I go walking through the gardens, I find tomatoes, peas, tender beans, baby lettuce, sweet beets and parsley growing in the oddest places. My arms become a salad bowl filled with delicious veggies I happily pop into my eager mouth.

I decided to offer the Quechua one *sol* (approximately thirty cents) for each unusual, living plant they brought me. The spiral garden filled with interesting native plants and medicinal herbs. Fabian and the gardeners explained their uses. With the passing months, the gardeners were happy to bring new flowers and medicinal plants we did not have at Willka T'ika.

They would not take money from me, saying
that they found the plants growing in the wilds
around their homes.

Knowing I had a lot to learn from the spiral, I
frequently walked its paths in silent meditation.
I knew this garden carried very special
energies. Consciously, I began asking Nature
for Her guidance. No longer needing to use
a pendulum, I would ask a question, and the
answer would come. The workers understood
the spiral was to be treated more gently than
agricultural fields. We had worked so hard to
prepare its precious topsoil. I did not want it
carried away by gushing water. I reminded
them not to flood the spiral with water the same
way they flooded their hardy crops.

Throughout the year, the spiral revealed
surprises. I recalled reading a spiritual garden
workbook written by an American woman.
Filled with tables and designs, the book
gave instructions for placing plants so they
would grow together. Gazing at the spiral's
eclectic plants, I wondered if I should look at
the information and apply it to the flowers.
Standing in the same area where I received the
first message to build a spiral, I heard, "Enjoy
yourself. Leave the books. Allow yourself to
have fun. There are no such rules in Nature.
Pachamama knows what to do, and we know

what to do as well. Do what brings you joy." The message was followed by light giggles. Smiling to myself, I was happy to be reminded that just as I had not needed an architect, building plans, contractors, engineers or landscapers to get me this far, I could forget about garden books and rules. All I had to do was remain open to the brilliant forces and invisible beings working alongside me in Nature.

By now, almost everything growing in the spiral was enhanced by shades of indigo and purple. Tiny flowers from rosemary plants and clusters of spring onion, petunias, pansies, scabiosa and ever-lasting statice appeared in those colors. Their petals were splashed with contrasting speckles of yellow, orange, white and red, bringing soft vibrations to each flower.

Spending time in the spiral energies seemed to make it easier for me to think consciously about ways to stay happy and healthy by living a wholesome lifestyle. I found it easier to attune to Nature. This enabled me to receive unlimited, inspirational ideas about what to do next. With greater clarity, I was able to continue my work in the gardens. I knew that guests who chose to walk in silent meditation could absorb healing vibrations from the flowers growing within the spiral energies.

A few years before my South African father passed away he handed me an envelope marked "Bearded Irises 1988," containing shriveled-up bulbs. Gardening was his hobby. Old home movies show me helping him in the garden from the moment I could walk. I never found time to plant them. A decade later, they reappeared from their hiding place in the back of a drawer in a piece of furniture I brought to Peru. I planted them in the center of the spiral. To my absolute delight, six months later, the bulbs burst into magnificent, lilac irises. I was deeply moved to see my father's lilac irises blooming in the center of the spiral in my garden in Peru, many years after he had passed away. For me, the irises were a gift to heal unresolved issues between us. My appreciation of the healing power of Nature became ingrained in my soul. Having multiplied many times since then, the offspring of the shriveled iris bulbs are planted throughout the spiral.

When I walked the spiral, I noticed plants and creepers growing in a spiral formation. Exotic vine fruits, tumba and granadilla, similar to the passion fruit family, and lilac sweat-peas displayed spiral growth in their movement toward the light. I realized this garden resonated deeply with my third-eye chakra,

the seat of clairvoyance and intuition. I felt this chakra opening as the spiral energies of Nature continued to enhance my intuitive abilities. Like the plants, I was thrilled to journey toward the light. In the Spiral Garden, I moved toward higher realms of consciousness.

Spending time in the spiral energies seemed to make it easier for me to think consciously about ways to stay happy and healthy while living a wholesome lifestyle...

Andean Lore and the Spiral Garden

The ancient Inka people believed that the *kuntur* (condor) represented the realm of spirit. Condors could, if they flew high enough, touch the life-giving Sun. From their perspective, condors viewed all three Andean worlds. They were regarded as messengers from the gods, heavens or upper world, hanakpacha. From its perspective in the upper world, high above the mountain peaks, the condor represents the ability to cut through illusion. "Fly like the condor, spiral up through the sky, into the universe."

The highest level of healer is the *kurakakulleq* (distinguished chewer of leaves). To attain this level, he has submitted to a rigorous initiation in the glaciers of the highest Andean mountain peaks where the energy of the earth is said to be concentrated. The authentic lineage of these initiated masters appears to have died out, but it is still possible to meet with an authentic *altomisayoq*, also called *apuche* or apukuntur. They are healers with the ability to leave the physical body and are often represented by the powerful symbol of the kuntur. In Andean towns, people gather in small rooms of houses to receive messages from the condor. Sessions are rather dramatic with darkness and incense adding tension to the atmosphere. The attending altomisayoq brings messages from the apukuna, mountain deities, to the people.

In the Spiral Garden, the condor resonates with the third-eye chakra. Vision is clear and sharp. Insights abound. The third eye leads people through illusion into clearer, higher consciousness

Authentic Andean healers operate from the third eye. Gifted healers, coca-leaf readers, psychics or clairvoyants can see through this center beyond the limiting horizons of time and space. The Spiral Garden resonates with the energies of healers and people who have open third-eye chakras.

The Spiral Garden's Third-eye Chakra

Situated between the brows and a little above, this chakra is known as the *ajna*, or third-eye chakra. Referred to as the seat of the mind, it is the energy center through which people consciously and unconsciously perceive themselves and the world around them. All information, impressions, sensations and emotions in the body are integrated in the third eye. It controls reactions to what is happening in their lives internally—through the nervous system, and externally—through their decisions and actions.

Images people have of the world are totally constructed in their minds. These images consist of information received from the outside world combined with their own assessments. Past experiences influence the mind's images.

Perception in this chakra goes beyond physical sight. Pure, balanced energies of the third eye, together with the other chakras, determine the quality and accuracy of people's views of themselves, the world around them and their interactions.

If the chakra is unbalanced, they may stumble blindly through life or live in an illusion that does not match reality. A balanced third eye allows them to walk forward with confidence in their own decisions and visions for their futures.

Human beings experience an ongoing and never-ending spiral journey through life. Reviewing the journey of the kundalini serpent of wisdom as it relates to the chakras and chakra gardens offers a clear understanding of how it spirals up through active and passive channels of energy in the physical, spiritual and psychic bodies. Moving from the nurturing earth energies, it gains fluid movement and suppleness from water energy, personal power from fire energy, loving intent from heart energy, integrity and joyful creativity from throat energy, and arrives at the third-eye energy center that brings inner vision and clear understanding. In this chakra Life energies come together to be refined, integrated and replenished with divine love, wisdom and power. This leaves people feeling in total command of their lives.

In the spiral of Nature, as people move toward the light, they become renewed and recharged. Each level of their life spiral presents experiences that are influenced by their ever-changing emotions and circumstances. The ways that they confront challenges and overcome discord are parts of their life journey.

Power of the Spiral Garden

When people stay connected to Pachamama, God or their Divine Source, they become empowered to use their spiritual resources to eliminate negativity. They transform their world from a state of limitation and fear to a state of abundance and love. The world is a reflection of humanity's collective consciousness. It has no separation or division. Pachamama teaches mankind to keep all things in balance. At times, She creates shifts in the Earth and presents mankind with challenges that get resolved as She returns to balance.

People often display obsessive drives for wealth, success or power, neglecting other aspects of themselves. Blocked third-eye energy is indicated by a blind acceptance of the beliefs and values of others, indecision and rigidity of thought and the pursuit of destructive relationships. People do not have to stay in this energy. They have a choice to realign themselves energetically with a life of peace and co-existence.

Spending time in this garden assisted Rhegina in realigning her energy: *"As I walked past the Spiral Garden, going back to my room, I heard the words very clearly, 'Walk the spiral.' I started. 'Take off your flip flops.' I took off my flip flops and started walking again. I felt a bit of tension in my stomach. It seemed to be the residue of an earlier worry. As I walked, the tension began to uncoil. Like a magnet, the energy pulled me to the left, spiraling into my center. Step by step, I relaxed and felt more grounded. I came to a narrow passage. 'Push through,' I heard clearly. It felt like the spiral was becoming a metaphor for my life, representing easy parts, tight spots, challenges and fears."*

Meditation in the Spiral Garden

The meditation symbol of the Spiral Garden is a triangle pointing upward. Mentally place the triangle above the third eye. Focus on the three points of the triangle. Breathe into the third eye and affirm: "Love, Power and Wisdom." Breathe out, feeling "Love, Power and Wisdom."

Recite silently or aloud:

"Great Spirit of the Condor,

Master beings of the Upper World,

please receive my prayer.

May I forever welcome love, power and wisdom into my life.

I am open to intuition and profound wisdom.

As I breathe in, I receive purity and balance in the third eye.

As I breathe out, I send clarity of vision out into the universe.

I am on a never-ending spiral journey to the light."

Allow yourself to go into a deep meditation.

Spiral Walking Meditation

Walk the spiral as a meditation to open up the energies of the third eye. "Walk slowly, coordinating your breath with your steps, and walk as if you are kissing the earth with your feet. Stepping with care, the path will lead you," said Thich Nhat Hanh, Buddhist monk and teacher. Practice his words on the spiral walk. When you walk this way, you bring peace and calm to Pachamama. You heal yourself and your Mother at the same time. Pause, and look deeply at a beautiful flower. Continue with focused breathing. Walk in the present moment. There is no need to arrive.

Enter the Spiral Garden prepared to integrate the awareness you have gained on your journey through the first five chakra gardens. By working through those chakras, you have gained perspective about where you are currently headed in your life.

Walk the spiral path toward the center of the garden, reviewing the course of your life up until now.

Throughout your life, similar experiences, both positive and negative, have repeated themselves as you followed a spiral course. You may not have recognized them as being comparable at the time, since each occurrence was surrounded by different circumstances.

🌹 At the center of the spiral, pause and reflect on what you have learned on your journey.

🌹 What messages has life been offering you?

🌹 Which aspects of your life do you wish to leave behind?

🌹 Which aspects of your life do you wish to take into your future?

🌹 Continue walking the spiral as it unwinds from the center.

You are effectively "unwinding" your past as you walk into the spiral and "winding up" your future as you walk out. You are bringing forth your desires for your future based on your fulfilled past.

🌹 As you walk out of the spiral, continue to release the energies you wish to leave behind.

🌹 Feel yourself reinforcing the aspects you wish to use in creating and building your future.

As you leave the spiral, you will feel refreshed and strengthened. You will have a new perspective on where your life is taking you. You will feel prepared to be fulfilled by it.

Lucuma

Tree Garden

Lucuma Tree Garden

Proudly standing as a metaphor for all creation, the ancient *lucuma* (*look-ma*) tree is a magical keeper of limitless power, wisdom and longevity. The Lucuma Tree Garden is a place of inspiration, spiritual vision and timeless Andean ritual. It resonates with the crown chakra.

Surrounded by pure-white flowers tinged with delicate strokes of gold and violet, this garden has energies that purify and center the soul. White is a brilliant vibration made up of all colors resonating in perfect harmony. They connect to the higher power of universal consciousness.

Crown Chakra:

Doorway to universal consciousness

Andean garden symbol:

Lucuma tree, a thousand-year-old tree of life; ancient teacher.

Primary color:

White, with touches of gold and violet

Meditation symbol:

Triangle pointed down. "I receive."

Signature Plant of the Crown Chakra Garden

Lucuma Tree

The lucuma tree at Willka T'ika is the grand maestro of the gardens. With each gnarled knot on its trunk representing over one hundred years, this ancient tree may be close to a thousand years old. The base of the fruit has a star pattern, symbolizing the cosmos or universe. Representing unity, the tree is a hermaphrodite. Greatly honored in Peru, the lucuma tree has twenty-six towns named after it. As the signature plant for the crown chakra garden, it captures its essence.

The golden, ripened fruit is heart-shaped. Ancient Peruvian ceramics dating as far back as 800 - 1,000 years B.C.E. are decorated with art depicting this fruit. This edible fruit is known to weigh up to two hundred grams, or almost half a pound. Once fertilized, fruit takes nine months, or ten new moons to ripen. The fruit is bright green. A few days before it falls to the ground, it turns golden. The lucuma fruit is a major source of vitamin C for Andean people. Extracts treat skin ailments. The leaves are used to dye fabric.

The beauty of this tree—with its small, tube-like, white flowers tinged with soft yellow and green; its rich orange fruit; shiny, mahogany seed; and emerald leaves—attracts attention and resonates with the crown chakra. Rooted in the earth while reaching toward the sun and moon this tree speaks of ancient memories.

It is believed to carry messages from ancestors. It reminds people of the possibilities of a joyful life. Meditation under the lucuma tree is said to help people remember past and present. Vibrationally, the lucuma connects people to universal, cosmic forces.

White Plants of the Lucuma Tree Garden

BEARDED IRISES

Magnificent, white, bearded irises in the Lucuma Tree and Spiral Gardens inspire people to put their creative ideas into practice. Meditating with this iris has helped me clear past issues. It inspired my endeavors to create the Chakra Gardens. I am reminded of my connection to my ancestors. We are one. It becomes clear that we are part of the same integral structure. The messages people often hear from flowers relate to joy. They remind us to be childlike. No matter where plants originate, they all come from the same Earth energy.

CALLA LILIES

Calla lilies grow wild and abundantly in the Sacred Valley. Their message reminds people of their inner purity. Vibrationally, they balance masculine and feminine energies, bringing clarity about sexual identity and self-respect.

CHAMOMILE

Every Quechua home grows dainty *manzanilla*, a favored chamomile plant with delicate, white flowers. Both leaves and flowers are used in herbal tea to soothe, calm and keep everyone healthy. Manzanilla is said to give people a sunny disposition. It is used not only for sleeplessness, digestive problems, gastritis and stomach ailments, but also for hay fever, asthma and eczema. Chamomile is known to ease emotional stress in the nervous system.

EASTER LILIES

In the Southern Hemisphere, Easter lilies, *asusena*, bloom in spring. Their beautiful, white flowers represent the purity of the soul and the integration of sexuality and spirituality. Easter lily vibrations make it possible for people to reconcile the feelings of tension between sexuality and spirituality. Flower essence remedies assist with disturbances in female sexual and reproductive organs.

SHASTA DAISIES

Easy to grow, Shasta daisies are found almost everywhere in this region. Meditating with them, or gazing at their profusion of silky, light-filled petals, assists with integrating the scattered activities of busy people into cohesive meaning. A popular affirmation for busy people is "I am a human be-ing," rather than a human doing.

KAPULI TREES

When I cleared the land around the old lucuma tree in 1994, I left in place four *kapuli*, or Andean cherry trees. Growing a few feet away from the ancient being, they appeared to be its guardians, shielding it from late afternoon winds and protecting its fragile bark. Native to the Cusco region, the kapuli, *prunus serotina*, offers shade, repels bugs, grows for decades, and self-seeds around Quechua homes. It never needs pruning or watering. Generations have relished its gifts and used them to prevent coughs and colds. Kapuli trees bring joy, laughter and nourishment to Quechua children. Each summer in the Sacred Valley, children easily climb the sturdy branches to reach ripened clusters of deliciously sweet, cherry-like fruit.

212 Lucuma Tree Garden

Creating the Lucuma Tree Garden

When I first set my eyes upon the lucuma tree in 1994, Pachamama's blueprint for the chakra gardens was in place. But I did not know that at the time. While the Quechua around me were chatting about where I should build my house and which parcel of land I should buy, my gaze remained transfixed by a spindly-looking ancient being, hidden behind piled-up dead scrub and burnt, thorny branches. No one had considered that I might find the old lucuma tree the most intriguing part of the land purchase. As the Quechua marched off to check the water supply, I moved toward the tree. Looking brittle and neglected at that first meeting, it was not physically appealing, but as I placed my hand on its knobby trunk, my heart told me I was meeting an old, much-loved friend. My soul connected with this ancient being I must have known in other lifetimes.

By the time the Quechua returned to assure me that *Lucmayoc* (place of the lucuma tree) could receive water from mountain streams above, I was ready to purchase the land. I did not care about its size or about negotiating the price. To the surprise of the sellers, I casually said, "I'll take it all." Just one meeting with the lucuma tree had left me with no doubt about the land or where I should live.

To live in Peru and purchase land, I needed to officially become a permanent resident. In Cusco, I patiently allowed the eager-to-earn-her-commission Quechua tour agent to lead me through a warren of Notary Public offices. There, I was shown immigration documents that made little sense to me. In crowded municipal offices, while the agent babbled away to officials on my behalf, I signed a mountain of documents that allowed me, as a foreigner, to purchase land in the Sacred Valley.

Eight months later, I received a message that my house was ready. Expecting to move right in, I was greeted by walls of mud covered by a roof and no plastered ceilings. After parting with a lot of money, with little to show for it, I decided I was ready to continue further construction on my own. Professionals I had hired proved to be uncommitted and inefficient. I designated myself supreme construction manager and set about building a yoga studio and new guest rooms for family and friends. Mark's role was to support me in my creative endeavors.

At seven each morning, the Quechua arrived punctually to work. I happily looked forward to each day, observing everything and learning from them. As I tapped into their rhythm and style of work, I became totally involved in everything around me. I no longer felt a stranger on my own land.

After months of camping in Andean mud, Mark and I moved into the luxury of a spacious, modern house with hot, running water.

While construction continued at the top end of the property, I moved around the lower end, guiding workers to clear and prepare the land for planting. Spending my days so close to the land, touching and feeling Her earthy elements, revitalized me. I accepted the challenges and enjoyed stomping around in my rubber boots amid the mud and stones while good-natured Quechua men helped me with all heavy work.

At noon each day, the workers went home for lunch. For five years, we had no telephone, television or internet connections. As a peaceful wave of silence swept over Willka T'ika, I sat in bliss under the lucuma tree and enjoyed a tranquil hour beneath its welcoming shade. Grateful to have my own Andean spiritual master teacher on site, I asked the lucuma, Pachamama and all the guardian spirits of that area for help in bringing me what I needed.

Within a short time, the right person or object would appear in my life. There was no doubt that Pachamama had a special plan for me. All I had to do was be present, open and trust it would unfold.

My frequent visits to the lucuma tree seemed to feed me with energy and creative ideas. I began with a simple prayer to connect with the spirit of the ancient tree. Each time I closed my eyes to meditate, I became conscious of the vibrations around my crown chakra and opened to receive spiritual energies.

The Lucuma Tree Garden became the first sacred garden at Willka T'ika. The Quechua helped me place stones to sit beneath the tree in its shade. With masses of dazzling, white flowers, bordered by emerald green grass, the garden sparkled like a brilliant oasis in a desert. Daily, I visited the tree and sat on a large rock that had "watched" the tree grow for so many years.

I continued to open my crown chakra consciously to receive whatever messages were being sent my way. I followed Pachamama's guidance, applying Her insights. As I gazed at the magnificent mountains in the distance, I was transported into a magical world that fed my soul and inspired my inner being.

The Lucuma Tree Garden remained a focal point of spiritual connection to the pure energies of the Sacred Valley. The old tree, referred to in Quechua as a *mallk*i (ancient, wise being), was anchoring the energy of the masses of flowers growing in the surrounding gardens.

After a recent visit overseas, I returned to greet the lucuma. The tree looked slightly shriveled, like a person who has lost a lot of weight. Its aura was gray. I was concerned that the recently-constructed, giant, yoga studio, the *Kuntur Runtu* (Condor Egg), might have been built too close to the lucuma tree. During a dry season years before, I had contemplated what would happen if the tree suddenly dried up and died. I believed without the tree, I would feel like I had lost a soul mate, and life at Willka T'ika would not be the same.

I called together the shaman, Don Benito and all the Willka T'ika staff. I invited them to participate in a special ceremony to honor and heal the Mallki. I requested that Benito ask the tree if it were suffering or in trouble. In over forty years, I don't believe Benito had ever read coca leaves on behalf of a tree. He and the Quechua staff remained extremely serious and respectful as I went ahead and asked questions.

I was greatly relieved when Benito pronounced,

My frequent visits to the lucuma tree seemed to feed me with energy and creative ideas...

"The lucuma tree is not drying up. The tree is most grateful to us all for taking such wonderful care of it over the years." He told us that the lucuma tree wanted people to continue to offer love, blessings and coca leaves in its garden. "Visitors ask a lot from the Mallki and Pachamama," he said, "but give little back in return." Like all living beings, the lucuma tree needed to be replenished with loving energy and positive vibrations. I made a mental note to remind guests to practice what I call "tree ayni." They must give love and respect to the lucuma tree to receive the same.

In answer to my final questions, the lucuma tree said it had adjusted its deep, extensive root system to accommodate the wonderfully energetic yoga studio, Kuntur Runtu. It was happy to be close to a place that would bring joyful vibrations. All it needed now, according to Don Benito, were two special offerings. One offering was to be dedicated to Pachamama, and another, a *tinkuy* (offering to honor old friends), to the surrounding mountain deities.

During that tinkuy ceremony, Benito bound our energies with those of the lucuma tree and Nature for the mutual benefit of all. Passion and enthusiasm poured out of him as he blessed Pachamama, the lucuma tree, the mountains, streams, flowers, people, animals, moon, sun, rainbow, ocean and Inkan gods. He blessed me, he blessed us all. I visualized the tree getting stronger. As Benito infused every living being with positive vibrations, love and strength flowed into the lucuma's spindly branches.

We learned the lucuma tree drew energy from the four great apukuna, mountain deities, and held the energies of the plants and living beings for miles around. There was no doubt that the

(clockwise from left,) Don Benito, fruit of the lucuma, nearby Apu Salkantay one of the great mountains honoring feminine energy

tree was almost one thousand years old. Each knot on the tree represented approximately one hundred years.

Each time a group came to stay, the lucuma tree dropped one or two bright-orange fruits from its branches onto the green grass below. Our Quechua chefs craftily baked the fruit into a delicious dessert. I reminded guests they were eating more than a thousand years of wisdom.

One quiet afternoon, I went to meditate beneath the lucuma tree. I looked up. About half-way up the trunk, I saw new, healthy-looking branches filled with emerald green leaves. They had sprouted since Benito's ceremony. The tree was showing us how much it appreciated the special blessings and attention it had received.

From the ancient Lucuma tree sprouts new life.

218 Lucuma Tree Garden

Andean Lore and the Lucuma Tree

The lucuma tree encompasses the three worlds of ancient Andean cosmology. The trunk represents *kaypacha*, the world of humans, plants and animals, a place of action and interaction, of cause and effect that shapes our lives. The roots represent *ukhupacha*, the inner world of wisdom and experience. The leaves and branches reach into *hanakpacha*, the upper world of spirit, of creative ideas and inspiration. All three interconnected realms create the world we live in.

Having awakened each energy center in the body, Amaru, the serpent goddess of the Inka, or kundalini energy, bursts through the crown energy center, opening it to spiritual enlightenment. Unrestricted by previous patterns, people become linked with cosmic energy, eternal wisdom and boundless inspiration. Life fills with passion. Wisdom becomes profound. Insights are infinite.

The lucuma tree connects everyone to this universal, cosmic consciousness. Gateway to the wisdom of the ages, the lucuma leads mankind toward spiritual fulfillment. By interacting with this ancient tree, people exchange living energy with all life. Profound inspiration can be revealed through our own minds to us. The lucuma tree is a living representative of the connection between Mother Earth and the cosmos.

In the Inkan language, "Mallki," also referred to their ancestors and ancient trees whose wisdom they honored. During that time, Willka T'ika's lucuma tree offered its nourishing fruit to Inka children living in the Sacred Valley.

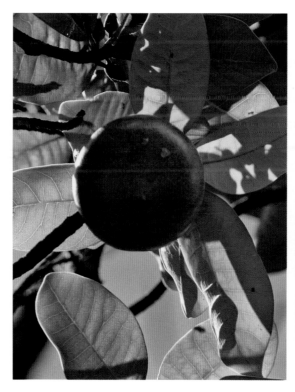

Review of the Crown Chakra

Situated at the top of the head close to the fontanel, the crown chakra—called a *pujyu*, or fountain by Andeans—is the place where body and soul come together. Spirit flows through it, giving life. Through the crown chakra, people can learn to transcend all that they have known.

The crown chakra opens the doorway to blissful energies of universal consciousness. People can transcend ideas of duality such as masculine versus feminine, dark or light, good and evil. Bliss is not a state that can be described; It must be experienced. When the crown chakra is open and balanced, people experience their wholeness. The mantra "I am," affirms the message of the crown chakra.

Humans are analogous to the lucuma tree. Nourished by Pachamama, their bodies constantly receive energy that moves through their chakras to be processed. Via thoughts, attitudes, inspirations and creativity, people contribute this energy to the universal consciousness. Through the life processes of receiving energy from the sun, nutrition from the earth and life force from the water, the lucuma tree is able to release its gift of oxygen and moisture into the atmosphere. Like the tree, if people do not take part in the creative cycle of receiving, processing and giving, they wither and die.

wall panel by Mario Jannco

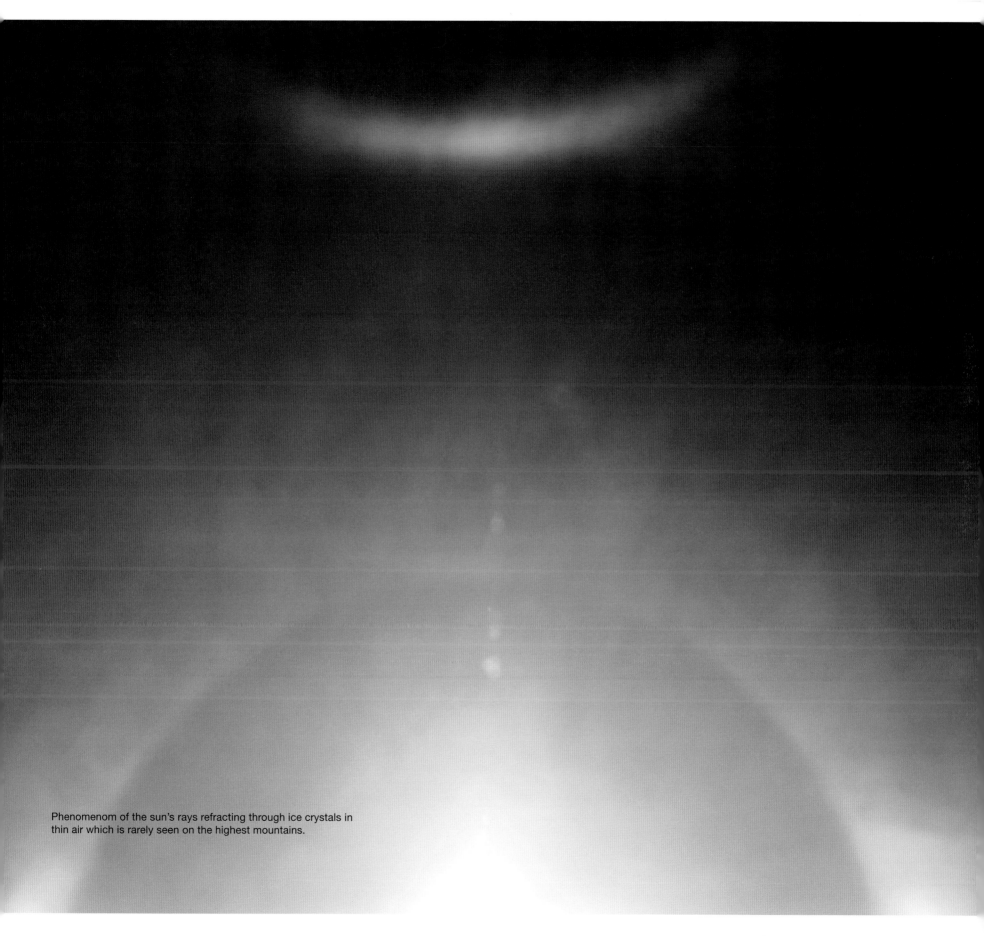

Phenomenom of the sun's rays refracting through ice crystals in
thin air which is rarely seen on the highest mountains.

Power of the Lucuma Tree Garden

I refer to the crown chakra as a "peace chakra." There are many ways to navigate life as a master of peace. People can train themselves not to allow chaos, world problems, family or friends to unbalance their crown chakra. Masters of peace do not allow unhealthy energy to attach to them. This does not mean they are disinterested or lacking in compassion. It is simply their choice not to allow stress, busyness or high drama to become part of their lives. Masters of peace do not need to deny what is happening around them. They simply focus on only things they want to become part of their lives.

Crown chakras begin to open when people slow down and understand that all living beings are interconnected. What affects one, affects all. Imagine leaders of the world following their spiritual practice with meetings and discussions aimed at peace and diplomacy. What would it take for them to listen to the wisdom of a spiritual leader like the Dalai Lama?

A journey through Willka T'ika's Chakra Gardens culminates at the ancient lucuma tree. Through an open crown chakra, people experience a direct connection with their Divine Source, or God. To feel this connection, it is essential to practice having a genuinely open and quietly accepting mind.

Nature's lesson for the crown chakra, and all the other chakras, is to be open, purified of extraneous influences and accepting of intuitive messages.

An Experience in the Lucuma Garden

A recent guest to Willka T'ika wrote;

"At the end of my first tour of the gardens, I was guided to a wise tree. Later, I learned it is more than eight hundred years old. Imagine what this being can tell you when you are ready. This beautiful soul has crystals embedded in it. When you place your hands above them, waves of energy, unconditional love and complete peace flow through you. A voice in my head said clearly, *'You do not need to translate the language of love. It is not about the material. You already know that. It is what you see with your heart that makes a difference. Today we begin to feed your soul.'* I have never forgotten that message. It was clear and simple. I think we may make spirituality and our quest much more complicated that it really needs to be. Beautiful gardens and a tree reminded me of what is important. A year later, I am still processing the amazing experiences I had the honor of experiencing at Willka T'ika. It doesn't take much to change a life."

Chakra gardens are gardens of peace. They do not restrict or impose. They simply support people in experiencing their own deep connection to Source. Under the peaceful lucuma tree, people receive inspiration through the crown chakra. With a quiet mind, pure energies from Source are received. In that moment, there are no world problems.

✿ Become the lucuma tree.

✿ Deep in the earth, feel your roots absorb nutrients.

✿ Let the nourishing energy move up through your trunk.

✿ Release oxygen and moisture through your branches and leaves as you reach to the sky.

✿ Take from the earth, and give to the heavens. Draw from the heavens, and give back to the earth.

✿ Enjoy the giving and receiving of tree ayni, exchanging living energy with your world.

✿ Create this new rhythm in your life.

Meditation in the Lucuma Tree Garden

Meditation offers a solution to problems. The meditative state is a natural state of mind. When people take time to make that state a regular part of everyday life no matter what they are doing, that natural state can be reached.

The following meditations, exercises and ceremonies can be done in any garden using a significant tree. All trees share the same characteristics and are interconnected with the whole.

Beneath the old lucuma tree, sense your deep connection to the totality of the universe. As life forces of Nature swirl around and within you, distance yourself from any fear or restless doubt. Allow guidance and protection from Nature to carry you into the serenity of light where new realms of possibility inspire you to live your life as you choose. With the support of Pachamama, experience being the creator of your life. Know you have equal access to the Divine Source and all there is

Meditation on the Triangle Pointed Down

Meditate upon the triangle pointed down as if it were placed above the crown chakra of your physical body. Visualize pure Source Energy pouring into the triangle through the crown chakra. Affirm: "I receive."

Breathing in, fill this chakra with light and inspiration.

Breathing out, direct light energy throughout your body.

Feel pure energy coming from the crown chakra through your third-eye chakra, throat, heart, solar plexus, sacral and root chakras. Visualize and feel this energy filling your entire body with pure spiritual light. Relax and feel your body vibrating with this light energy.

Beloved lucuma tree,

great master of Pachamama's gardens,

please hear my prayer.

All that you are, I am.

All that I am, you are.

I am the light, love,

beauty and wisdom that you are.

So be it. Amen.

"I Am" Meditation

As you sit beneath the tree, make positive, "I Am" statements. Remain focused on the emotional feelings they generate. Sense your deep connection to the totality of the universe. Allow the forces of Nature to swirl around and within you as you are steered away from any fear or restless doubt.

Pachamama's guidance and protection carry you into the serenity of light. When you feel peace and vibrations of love, you are in the place of wholeness. You are one with your Divine Source. New realms of possibility inspire you to live your life as you choose. As the creator of your life, you access Divine Source.

The Spirit of the San Pedro Cactus

An Ancient Initiation Ceremony

An ancient initiation ceremony joyfully awakens the Spirit of San Pedro Cactus in the gardens of Willka T'ika. Historians have investigated San Pedro drawings taken from ancient textiles and pre-Columbian ceramic art. They confirm that this ceremony is more than two thousand-years-old.

During a day of rituals, in an environment of peace, a tall San Pedro Cactus growing in an open garden near to the chakra gardens, is lovingly dressed in *papacho* clothing. Papacho means, from the Earth. An antique poncho, *chullu*—hat, *chuspas*—woven purses filled with coca leaves, and *chumpis*—woven belts, adorn this sacred plant. After a light fast, initiates prepare a magnificent garland made from brilliant yellow flowers representing Inti, the Sungod. Filled with light, Inti brings personal power and abundance to all participants.

At Willka T'ika, Dr Papacho, a qualified naturopath and Peruvian healer, utters special prayers to awaken the spirit of the plant, and open "its" eyes. Strong medicinal powers initiate guests who have learned some of the magical secrets of ancient Inkan Medicinal plants. In a calm setting with no outside distractions, pilgrims chewing coca leaves dance joyfully around the dressed San Pedro cactus, twelve times in each direction. Placing the chewed coca leaves on white paper, Dr Papacho offers individual guidance on health and personal issues. The ceremony is closed with further prayers of thanks to Pachamama, and the apukuna. The spirit of San Pedro Cactus is left to rest until another ceremony takes place.

This joyful ceremony is meant to empower initiates and leave them with spiritual guidance and wisdom. It defines individual life choices and offers strict rules on how to proceed on the spiritual path. In ancient times, San Pedro cactus was regarded as one of the gifted sons of Pachamama. Today, the ancient sacred San Pedro plant ceremony is forgotten. It is not known by Qero pakkos or Quechua healers, and differs from San Pedro ceremonies practiced by healers in Northern Peru. At no time is the plant cooked and swallowed as a psycho-active liquid. After 500 years, the ceremony still appears to be a threat to the leaders of churches operating all over Peru. The authentic prayers used by Dr Papacho are guarded to preserve this sacred ritual.

Creating Your Own

Chakra Gardens

Embrace the Spirit of Nature that lies within you. Allow yourself a journey into higher realms of consciousness. With no outside distractions, the mind becomes quiet. Profound spiritual work is set into motion.

The Spirit of the Chakra Gardens

Willka T'ika's gardens are a conscious attempt to create an environment where everything is balanced and supportive. Nature meets people at their level and draws them to wherever they must go.

There is no competition in the garden. Flowers, insects, birds, dogs and humans live in harmony. Chakra gardens are free of religious dogma. With no specific formula to follow, they remind visitors that Pachamama's natural health and well-being are available to everyone. Every living being can experience their connection to a greater intelligence. It may take just a flash or a moment for guests to sense something important to their wholeness. Within the peaceful chakra gardens, guests are encouraged to focus on any healing they wish to experience.

Since Nature appears to be "out there," many people do not notice it or take time to appreciate it deeply. They discuss the weather, tornadoes and natural disasters as if they are separate entities, disconnected from their own energy field. Human beings are fields of energy like everything in nature: flowers, trees, animals, birds, insects and crystals dug from rocks. Without consciously knowing it, when people allow Nature to guide them, they activate positive changes. Bursts of luminous color vibrations from flowers, and all of Nature, can dissolve their problems.

Willka T'ika's Chakra Gardens do not stand alone. Healing is supported by freshly harvested, organic, vegetarian food. The garden guesthouse is mindful of its environment. With the right intention of friendly staff, energetically powerful gardens remind guests to find their spirit within. They are empowered to take responsibility for their own healing and the healing of the Earth.

Participation in ancient practices or programs such as yoga, meditation, qi-gong, chakra therapies and others are designed to keep energy flowing within the body system. This energy flow is a pathway to universal awareness and wellness. When these practices are consciously brought into Nature's energies, they are broadened and deepened in every dimension.

Let go of busy-ness

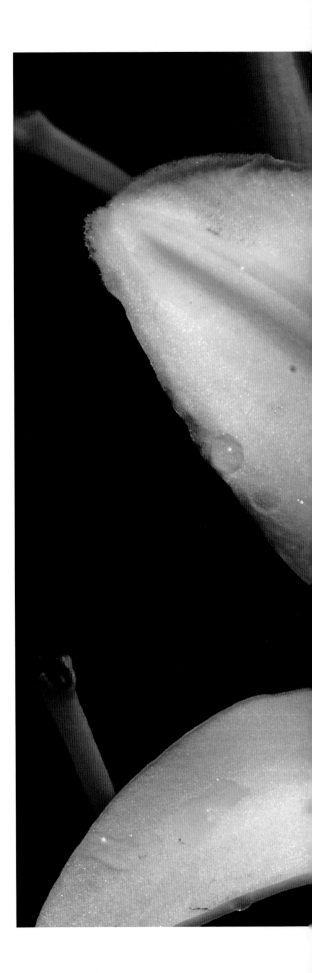

Most people in Western countries live their daily lives in a frenzy of activity. They may find they are so busy they don't allow themselves time "to be." When we allow everyday issues of the physical world to overtake us, imbalances and potential problems are created in body, mind and spirit. Under these conditions, Nature's pure, expansive vibration is prevented from entering and balancing the body through the chakras.

Let go of the busy-ness, and allow time to sit in chakra gardens. Pachamama's spiritual worlds are easier to feel, see, sense and experience when time is set aside to connect consciously with Nature.

Creating Your Own Chakra Gardens

The order in which you establish your chakra gardens is not important. Trust you will know where to begin. No two gardens on earth are alike. Nature has a design in mind for your garden.

Be mindful of your own physical limitations. If you have gardeners to help you, be ambitious. Otherwise, choose something that is simple to plant and easy to maintain.

Observe your surroundings. Make sure you are not too close to power lines, street noise or neighbors' dogs. Choose areas that will offer you privacy. Sit quietly in a place that draws you. Use your breath to connect you to Pachamama. Ask nature spirits to guide you on this exciting, creative adventure. Use a prayer or your own words to feel a connection to Nature, to Source energies.

If you do not have a garden, consider a patio or balcony. Clay planters filled with colored flowers, tiny cacti, or herbs can represent different chakras. Meditate and ask Nature for guidance. Place your intent within each flower planter, surrounding them with sacred objects or crystals that resonate.

If you have indoor living space only, be creative. Place seven small vases or bowls on a table, and bring in different colored flowers or fruits from your local organic market. Receive their fresh vibration, and feel the plant resonating with a particular chakra in your body. Frequently eat fresh, organic fruits and vegetables that encompass the rainbow colors of the chakras.

State your intentions for your chakra gardens. Focus on your intent. Trust you will make the right choices. In time, you will know which chakra resonates with the area you enjoy visiting. Specific colors will come to you. Observe plants growing in the area.

Whether you plant from scratch or choose an area filled with growth, ask Nature for guidance. Listen for the answers. At first, you might purchase a pendulum to ask yes-or-no questions. Accept insights and act on them. The more you meditate in your garden and connect to Nature's elements, the more you become aware of the guidance offered.

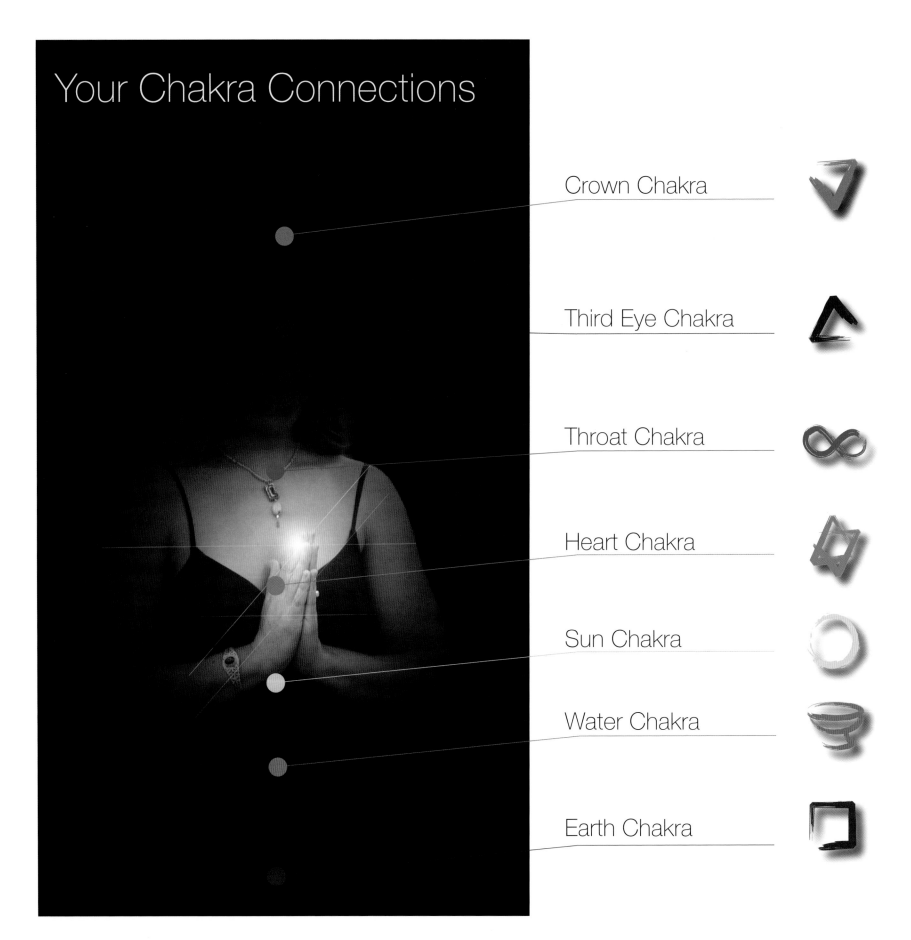

Your Chakra Connections

Crown Chakra

Third Eye Chakra

Throat Chakra

Heart Chakra

Sun Chakra

Water Chakra

Earth Chakra

Your Chakra Gardens

In each garden, introduce symbols, flowers, herbs and stones that are meaningful to you and relate to specific chakras. You may use well-illustrated garden books to find flowers of certain colors specific to your area. Or, use Andean symbols described in this book.

Following are some specific suggestions as you work with each chakra in your garden.

EARTH (PACHAMAMA)

Look for an area that reminds you of the Earth, Her rich soil, boulders, vines and tones of red. Can you see a snake symbol fitting into that garden? Bring your attention to your root chakra. Does it feel like you are connected to the earth? Breathe in the earth through this chakra. Do you feel protected?

WATER (YAKU)

Is there natural water? Or, are you feeling inspired to build a water feature? If "yes" to either question, your water garden already knows its place. Bold orange and cactus plants may fit right in. Perhaps an orange tree already sits there. Feel a flow of energy moving into your sacral chakra. Stay in the flow of life.

SUN (INTI)

Study the path of the sun. Where does it shine most of the day? Consider that area to be a sun garden. Can you visualize your sun garden filled with yellow flowers? Feel the warmth of the sun. Feel its light pouring into you. Feel its heat and fire in the solar plexus. Take in its "puma energy" or your own symbol of power and strength.

HEART (SONQO)

Allow yourself to find a gentle area where love pours into your heart. Close your eyes. Feel your heart expanding. Visualize the garden filled with verdant green leaves, soft pink blossoms or cascading flowers. Picture your pets visiting and insects buzzing around. Feel completely at peace. Allow loving vibrations from Nature to embrace you as you send love to Her. There will be no doubt that this is the love garden when a stream of pure love enters and leaves your heart in Heart Ayni, an exchange of loving energies.

THROAT OR SOUND (TAKIWASI)

Where in your garden, do you feel like singing, humming or chanting? In that place, joyful energy will come to you. Visualize blue and turquoise plants encouraging you to speak your truth to the world. Allow yourself to become more of who you really are.

THIRD-EYE (SPIRAL)

Ask first—then listen carefully—for guidance about where to build a spiral that mirrors your life and Nature. Pachamama's design will be given to you to suit your own space. A spiral garden could be a vegetable garden planted around a mound, a miniature garden or a giant walking spiral, similar to Willka T'ika's spiral. Allow it to evolve as Pachamama spirals with you. Watch lilac, indigo and violet-hued flowers come your way. As your third-eye opens, receive sparks of intuition. Live your expanded vision for life.

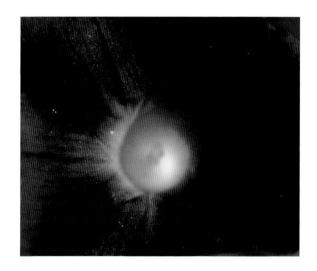

CROWN (LUCUMA TREE)

Seek your own ancient tree, sacred plant or holy place where you feel more connected to the Divine. Visualize yourself in a garden of brilliant white flowers. Sit in deep meditation, and open your crown chakra to receive inspirational energies from the Universe. Feel your connection to Source. Relax into that pure stream of energy as it fills and spiritually nurtures your body.

Enjoying Your Chakra Gardens

Over time, energies in chakra gardens expand. Pause, and look at all that surrounds you. Gaze deeply at a pebble, leaf or blade of grass. Notice its surrounding light. Close your eyes, and feel sensations in your body. Listen to Nature's sounds. Breathe in Her fragrances. Trust, and in time it becomes easy to sense the energy.

As each harmonious space fills with flowers and healing herbs, tiny creatures and birds will arrive to balance the energies. You may feel, or see, your gardens inhabited by garden spirits and illumined by ethereal energies. Express gratitude and appreciation for the beauty that surrounds you. Talk to your growing plants. Encourage them, and admire their beauty. Send them love. Your positive and loving vibrations bring magnificent beauty into form. Observe how flowers uplift your spirit. See them respond to praise. Ask questions of them, and listen for answers. Pachamama's vibrant flowers, insects, birds and stones work together to energize each garden.

Acknowledge the garden you have chosen. Find a comfortable place to sit. Consider making a simple offering to Pachamama. At Willka T'ika, She receives coca leaves. Choose your own cultural plant offering to Mother Earth.

Chakra Gardens are ongoing, forever changing. As you make changes in your life, you may feel drawn to doing the same in each garden. Remember, there are no rules. Feel free to move stones and paths. Replant flowers. Allow your creative spirit to lead you.

Walk mindfully along garden paths. Feel the joy when you observe flowers growing amidst rocks, dancing butterflies and insects. Allow yourself to go wherever you feel drawn.

Close your eyes. Be still. Listen to the sounds in Nature. Let the color of each garden, or a rainbow of colors, flow through your body. Enjoy each sensation. Trust that Nature and the surrounding flowers are sending you the color vibrations you need.

Meditate for as long as you are comfortable. Pay attention to your body. Observe how you feel in any given moment. As you continue to relax and breathe, allow yourself to receive Nature's soothing vibrations. When ready, open your eyes.

Breathe in gently but deeply. Relax as you feel the pure energies of Nature seep into your soul. Connect your breath with the rhythm of the earth. Know that you are safe, protected, surrounded by light. Call on the light forces of Nature. Ask your own spirit teachers to assist you. Ask Nature questions that are important to you. Ask for guidance. The answers will come.

Pachamama continues to send healing vibrations. In Her wisdom, She harmonizes chakra energies. Allow Her to enhance, balance and heal your body and surroundings. In return, express gratitude and admiration for what manifests in your garden. This is Chakra Ayni. Only when you find that place—away from the distractions of your mind and the world—can healing begin.

Rebalancing the Earth

By creating chakra gardens around the world, we can facilitate the rebalancing of the Earth. Each individual garden is like an acupuncture point on Pachamama's body. By sending love and appreciation to Her through gardens around the world, we send energy to realign and revitalize Her entire system. We will no longer just be taking from Her. We will also be giving to Her. We will be practicing Earth Ayni.

Love Nature with all your heart

In the gardens, allow yourself to become a child. You might even see and hear the elemental world of flowers. Express gratitude for the beauty that surrounds you. Greet the herbs and trees and acknowledge their exquisite design and beauty. Play with the flowers. Relax next to them and chat. Close your eyes and listen for messages. When insects approach, send them love. Laugh with small critters and smile at the bugs. They do not wish to harm you. Listen to the bird songs. Splash your face, hands and feet in the clear stream. Taste the ripe fruit. Feel the glorious warmth of the sun on your back. Allow the bees to do their work. Place your hands into the soft earth. Walk without shoes and feel the warm soil under your feet. Dance with bare feet on the morning dew. Salute the moon and walk on paths at night. Acknowledge the white flowers illuminated by the light of the stars and moon. Hum a soft tune.

When you love Nature so much, plan to sleep outdoors beneath the stars. Send offerings in a fire. Filled with the wonders of Nature, you begin to trust. Like a child, you begin to communicate with the plants and earth again. Write your own poem. Note how you feel. Create your own rituals for each garden. Gather any seeds you find or discard from fruit and vegetables you eat. With a blessing, press them into the soil as an ongoing offering to Pachamama. Mother Earth has aged over time, but she is immortal. As the earth gives you life, understand that you too are immortal. Death does not exist. Your consciousness lives forever.

Pure flower essences of each chakra garden help you rejuvenate. They assist you on your journey. Make sure your earth is living, just as she lives at Willka T'ika. Everything is alive, everything has meaning. Colors, wind, rain and rocks all speak to you. Nature, through your chakras, helps you move into your inner world, the source of all living experiences. When you enter a place like Willka T'ika, the beauty of Nature feeds the beauty within yourself – your inner garden flourishes. Make this part of your daily world by creating your own Chakra Gardens at home. Please share your own special story with us. Let us know of your progress.

Carol Cumes, info@chakragardens.com

Connect with Chakra Gardeners Around the World

Nature has no borders. Consciously created gardens raise the vibrational level of this planet. The author hopes all gardens created with this intention become energetically linked worldwide.

Please email us about your garden – info@chakragardens.com.

Share about your garden's progress, your name, city and country. We will add it to a map of chakra gardens linking us all together. If you have a brief, personal account of a transforming experience in your own chakra gardens that is meaningful to you, please email it to us. We may include it on our website. Helpful stories or hints to assist others on their healing journeys may be selected to appear in the next Chakra Gardens book.

Focus on an Earth that is perfect, pure and clean. Allow your energy to attract what you desire. When you see something stagnant, contaminated or spoiled, visualize it returning to life and beauty. Visualize the beauty of your garden as you wish it to be. At night in bed, send Pachamama "pictures" of your gardens. Nature will respond in magnificent ways that will surprise you.

Besides fulfilling the needs of the gardener, organic, self-sustaining energy gardens are the ultimate way of taking care of Earth's precious resources. With positive intentions, working closely with Pachamama benefits all mankind.

Our Willka T'ika staff (left to right) Fabian Hancco, Arturo Hancco, Lucio Cabrero, Antonia Jancco, Moises Sega, Carol Cumes, and Livio Sega

Acknowledgments

Thank you to Sidney and Frieda Franklin, for bringing me into a world filled with flowers, beautiful gardens, Kwazulu Natal's ocean and the wondrous game reserves of South Africa.

To Mark Hennessy, my wonderful partner, who, during 13 years of unending support and love, encouraged me to use my creativity and gave me the freedom to do so, my deepest thanks and love.

My appreciation includes the original Quechua gardeners of Willka T'ika—Fabian Hancco, Lucio Cabrero and Livio Sega—who helped me plant the Chakra Gardens. Thank you—Antonia Jancco, Arturo Hancco, Moises Sega, Julian Sega, and Florencio Franco—for managing and taking care of Willka T'ika, allowing me time for other projects. I am grateful to friends Gabriela Meneses, and Doris Riveros, who reads coca leaves. Both stay deeply connected to Pachamama. Together, with Qero Don Benito, we have laughed and had fun with the Andean spirit world.

My first spiritual teacher, Verna V. Aridon Yater, Ph.D., passed away in Santa Barbara on March 21, 2008. Verna, who fully supported the work at Willka T'ika, visited me many times. In a reading, she said an editor would come. In perfect time, Terranda King came to Willka T'ika and offered to edit the book without pay. Terranda did a magnificent and generous job of editing copious notes and chapters about the Chakra Gardens. Later in the year, Shawn Lewis joined her at Willka T'ika, and together they began a fabulous job of editing the book, from start to finish.

Humberto Valdivia visited from Lima and offered to capture the spirit of the gardens photographically, as did others, Keith Levit, Lee Kraemer and Shera Street. With so many people contributing at no charge, it was fitting that all proceeds of this book should benefit the Quechua Children's Fund.

Greg Asbury arrived as a guest at Willka T'ika in June 2007. Immediately, he was captivated by the Chakra Garden concept. He offered his services as a photographer and creative director. To capture the essence of the gardens photographically during summer solstice, Greg returned to Willka T'ika in December. Thank you to Greg and his company, Mitra Publishing Group in Sierra Madre, for publishing this beautiful coffee table edition.

Thank you, R. D. Chang, for confirming almost perfect feng shui in the gardens. We opened some energy pathways and never looked back. Thanks to my friend and naturopath, Dr. Papacho, for his enthusiastic acknowledgment of the magical healing potential of each garden and his contribution to my deeper understanding of Andean medicinal plants. My training in Flower Essences with Patricia Kaminski and Richard Katz in the eighties set the stage for Willka T'ika Chakra Garden essences I made over summer solstice in 2007. Yoga teacher training with Tracey Rich and Ganga White, and workshops with Patabhi Jois at the White Lotus in Santa Barbara over two decades ago, have served me well. Deep appreciation is extended to guests who contributed personal stories, to Annette Long and friend who read the manuscript and provided feedback, and to hundreds of guests, who over the years have enjoyed the gardens and infused them with loving energy. Thank you, Pachamama, for bringing wonderful people to Willka T'ika to help make this book possible.

Glossary

ajna (Sanscrit): third-eye chakra; center of light; seat of clairvoyance and intuition.

akkha (chicha) (Sp.): A thick, beige-colored, fermented drink made of germinating maize kernels; plays an important role in ceremonies and festivals.

altomisayoq: Andean healer or specialist

Amaru: the Inkan serpent; associated with the root chakra

apukuna: Andean deities; mountain protector spirits

arrieros (Sp.): muleteers

ayni: spirit of reciprocity; the Andean practice of giving and receiving; the belief in the wisdom that man benefits from helping others; love

baños (Sp.): baths

campesinos (Sp.): farmers

ceques: lines of energy in the land; ley lines

ch'ampa: thick-growing grass; sod

ch'askamayu: river of stars, or "Milky Way"

chakana: Andean cross; a multi-stepped, cosmological representation of the three Andean worlds

chakras (Sanscrit): wheels or vortices centered in the human body which generate vibrational energy that connects with energy fields outside the physical body

chicha (Sp.): also called akkha, a fermented drink made of corn, or maize.

choclo de oro: "corn of gold;" a flower shaped like a corn cob in shades of gold and orange

curandero (Sp.): healer

espiral (Sp.): spiral

faenas (Sp.): farming work cooperatives

hanakpacha: upper world of Andean cosmology; the world of divinity symbolized by the condor

haywarikuy: literally, "let us play;" a ceremony in which a healer sends special offerings of gratitude to Mother Earth in return for which she keeps the earth in balance allowing people to live in peace and harmony

Inkakuna: Inca people

Inti: Sun god

k'kayka: Quechua word for the clap of thunder produced by lightning; the sound of the word embodies the meaning.

kausay: living energy; yogic prana; chi; in the Andes, the energy that gives life

kaypacha: the physical world of humans, animals, plants in Andean cosmology; symbolized by the puma

kuka k'intu: a brief offering of coca leaves to the Andean deities, Pachamama (Mother Earth) or the apukuna (mountain spirits)

kundalini (shakti) (Sanscrit): primal energy

kuntur runtu: Condor egg; also, name of a yoga studio at Willka T'ika

kuntur: condor

kurakakulleq: highest level of healer; literally, "distinguished chewer of leaves"

layka: female healer

llipt'a: a small piece of lime ash, which releases the alkaloids from chewed coca leaves, acting as a soft stimulant

Lucmayoc: place of the lucuma tree; location of the crown chakra garden at Willka T'ika

lucuma: a large, round, unusual-tasting fruit that can be made into a custard-like dessert; also, name of the tree from which the fruit comes

mallku (mallki): ancient, wise being; ancestor, master, Andean teacher

mantra (Sanscrit): sacred sounds

mate(s): herbal tea(s)

munay: love

nina: the Andean spirit of fire

ninawasi: an indoor structure to honor fire

Pachamama: Mother Earth or Nature; the divine feminine

pajcha: fountains

pakkos or pakkokuna: professional Andean ritual specialists who conduct ceremonies to Pachamama. Shaman or medicine man.

palta: avocado

para-para: Quechua word for falling raindrops; the sound embodies the meaning

patuta: giant, spiral-shaped, conch shell used by the Inka as a musical instrument; vibrant red-orange, it is used like coral in jewelry phukuy: the blowing of one's essence on a coca leaf offering to the divine energies of Source

picaflores (Sp.): hummingbirds

picchar kuka: the act of chewing coca leaves

prana (Sanscrit): life-force energy; upward-moving vitality

pranayama (Sanscrit): the science of working with the energy of the body

pujyu: sacred springs

puma (Sp.): an Andean lion symbolizing power and courage

Pumawanka: place of the puma

qero: goblet

Quechua (Kkechuwa): name for both the indigenous Andean people and the language they speak

raki: ceramic pot

ruda (Sp.): Rue; a yellow-flowered, Andean plant of protection and abundance; used to assist with altitude sickness

sara: the name for Andean corn used in sacred ceremony

sequias: furrows, or open canals for channeling water.

sol: Peruvian coin worth approximately thirty cents; literally "sun"

sonqo: heart

sorroche (Sp.): altitude sickness

takiwasi: house of sound

tampu: resting place

Tawantinsuyo: the Andean world extending from Argentina to Colombia

tinkuy: offering to honor old friends

trono (Sp.): throne

ukhupacha: the lower, or hidden, inner world in Andean cosmology, represented by the serpent; inner earth

ukuña: ceremonial woven cloth; often used as a medicine bundle for healing purposes

waynas: songs that have been passed down for centuries

wayra: the wind that flows from the north

Willkamayu: Sacred River; the Urubamba River, also known today as the Vilkabamba River or Vilkanota River

Willka Bamba: Sacred Valley

Willka T'ika: "Sacred Flower;" a red, trumpet-shaped flower; name of the garden guesthouse and retreat center in the Sacred Valley of Peru

willka: sacred

yaku: water

Yakumama: Mother Spirit of water

yakuñawi: water spring

Arewa, Caroline Shola. *Thorsons Way of Chakras.* Hammersmith, London: Harper Collins, 2001.

Balbi, Mariela. *Lucuma, un legado de sabor prehispanico.* Peru, Enotria, 2003

Brown, Deni. *Encyclopedia of Herbs.* New York, NY: Dorling Kindersley, 1994.

Buhner, Stephen Harrod. *Sacred Plant Medicine. The Wisdom in Native American Herbalism.* Rochester, VT: Bear & Company, 1996.

Chopra, Deepak. *Synchro-Destiny.* Houghton, South Africa: Random House, 2005.

Cope, Stephen. *Yoga and the Quest for the True Self.* New York, NY: Bantam Books, 1999.

Cowan, Eliot. *Plant Spirit Medicine.* Columbus, NC: Swan Raven & Co., 1995.

Cumes, Carol. Lizarraga, Romulo. *Journey to Machu Picchu: Spiritual Wisdom from the Andes.* Cusco, Peru: Magical Journey, 2005.

Davies, Brenda. *The Rainbow Journey: Seven Steps to Self Healing.* Great Britain: Hodder & Stoughton, 1998.

Emoto, Masaru. *The Hidden Messages in Water.* Hillsboro, OR: Beyond Words Publishing, 2004.
Website: www.masaru-emoto.net or www.hado.net

Hanh, Thich Nhat. *Touching Peace: Practicing the Art of Mindful Living.* Berkeley, CA: Parallax Press, 1992.

Hansen, Bente. *The New World of Self-Healing.* Woodbury, MN: Llewellyn, 2006.

Kaminski, Patricia. Katz, Richard. *Flower Essence Repertory.* Nevada City, CA: The Flower Essence Society, 1994.

Pienaar, Kristo. *The Southern African: What Flower is That?* Cape Town, South Africa: Struik, 2001.

Roberts, Margaret. *Herbal Teas for Healthy Living.* Claremont, South Africa: Spearhead, 2005.

Roersch, C. *Plantas Medicinales en el sur Andino del Peru vol 1.* Cusco, Peru: Centro de Medicina Andina BUHO

Roersch, C. *Plantas Medicinales en el sur Andino del Peru vol 2.* Cusco, Peru: Centro de Medicina Andina BUHO

Rudd, Carol. *Flower Essences: An illustrated Guide.* Shaftesbury, Great Britain: Element Books Inc., 1998.

Simpson, Liz. *The Book of Chakra Healing.* New York, NY: Sterling Publishing, 1999.

Thomson, Donna, *The Vibrant Life: Simple Medications to Use Your Energy Effectively.* Boulder, CO: Sentient Publications, 2006.

Villoldo, Alberto. *Shaman, Healer, Sage: How to Heal Yourself and Others with the Energy Medicine of the Americas.* New York, NY: Harmony Books, 2000.
Website: www.fourwinds.com

White, Ganga. *Yoga Beyond Belief: Insights to Awaken and Deepen Your Practice.* Berkeley, CA: North Atlantic Books, 2007.

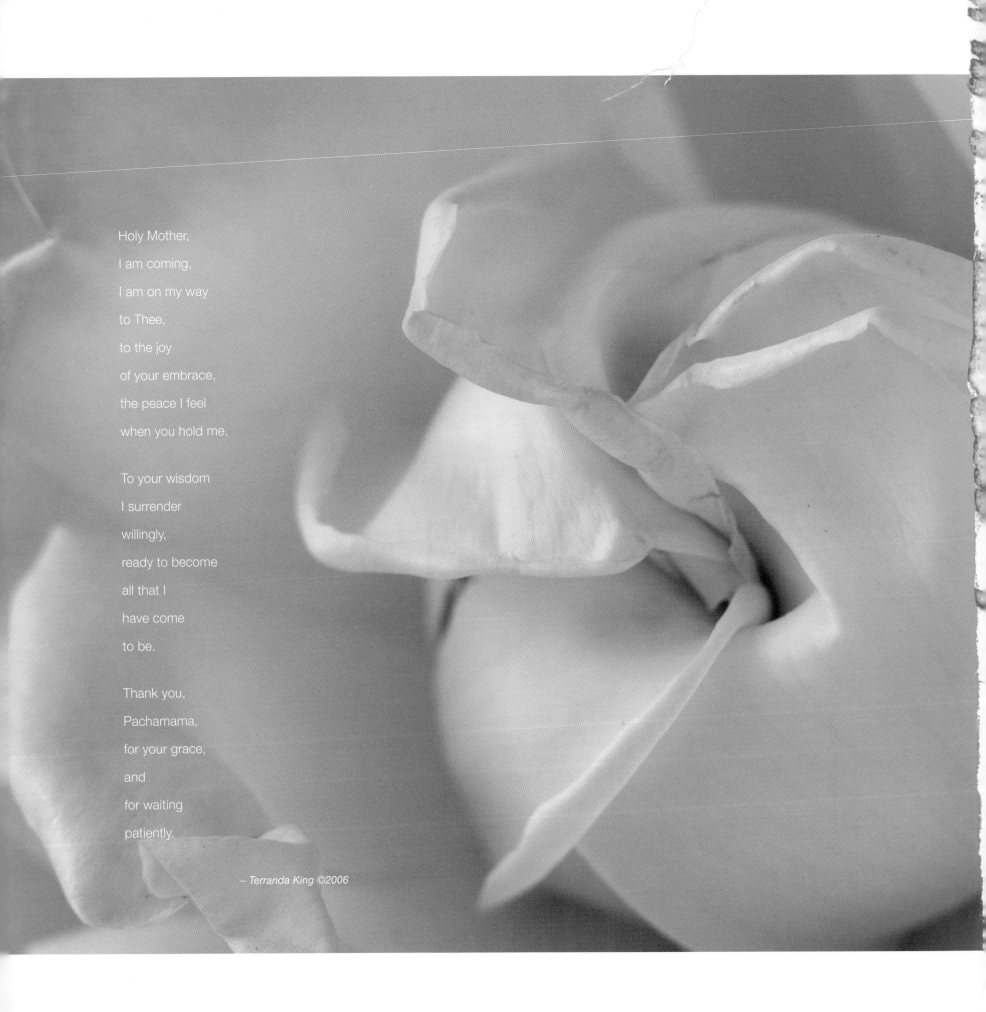

Holy Mother,

I am coming,

I am on my way

to Thee,

to the joy

of your embrace,

the peace I feel

when you hold me.

To your wisdom

I surrender

willingly,

ready to become

all that I

have come

to be.

Thank you,

Pachamama,

for your grace,

and

for waiting

patiently.

~ Terranda King ©2006